THE OVERNIGHT RÉSUMÉ

Donald Asher

Ten Speed Press

Ten Speed Press
P.O. Box 7123
Berkeley, CA 94707

Text and cover design by Fifth Street Design, Berkeley, California.

Library of Congress Cataloging-in-Publication Data

Asher, Donald.
    The Overnight Résumé/Donald Asher
        p.   cm.
    Includes bibliographical references.
    ISBN 0-89815-381-6 :
    1. Résumés (Employment)   I. Title.
HD5383.A84   1990
650.14–dc20

Printed in the United States of America

        3   4   5   —   95   94   93   92

A Note from the Author

The only significant difference between people who do things and people who don't is exactly that. Pick up this book and do something to make your life better.

— Donald Asher

Résumé Righters
625 Market Street
San Francisco, California 94105
(415) 543-2020

To my staff: Kathy Priola, Penelope Bell, Kathleen Docherty, Robin Klayman, Patricia O'Keefe, Christine Lee, Kimberly Brown, Joe Caffall, Lisa Lenker, Susan Hall, Rich Matheson, Frank Antonelli, Michelle Frame, Jim Targonski, Leigh Hancock. Nobody ever had a better staff.

To my clients, who taught me all the best tricks.

Table of Contents

Preface	How to Use This Book	*vii*
Chapter 1	Why You Need a Résumé	*1*
Chapter 2	What Your Résumé Can Do for You	*3*
Chapter 3	The Rules of Résumé Writing	*5*
Chapter 4	Résumé English Simplified	*7*
Chapter 5	Writing Your Résumé: Style Overview	*9*
Chapter 6	Writing Your Résumé: The One Thing You MUST Do First	*13*
Chapter 7	Writing Your Résumé: Getting Started with the Heading	*17*
Chapter 8	Writing Your Résumé: Win or Lose in the First Ten Lines	*21*
Chapter 9	Writing Your Résumé: Jobs and Dates	*25*
Chapter 10	Writing Your Résumé: Education and Additional Data	*35*
Chapter 11	Writing Your Résumé: Putting It Together	*41*
Chapter 12	Special Styles, More Tricks	*61*
Chapter 13	How to Get Interviews; How to Plan and Manage a Job Search	*81*
Chapter 14	Cover Letters: Don't Write One Until You Read Chapter 13	*93*
Chapter 15	Go For It! This Is Your Life	*105*
Appendix	Annotated Bibliography of Career Books	*107*

Preface
How to Use This Book

If you want to have your résumé ready by 9 A.M. tomorrow, skip the rest of this prologue, read only the parts of the book with a grey bar down the edge of the page, and get started right now. DO NOT SKIP CHAPTER 3, "The Rules of Résumé Writing."

This book makes several assumptions about you, the reader. In order to best evaluate whether the book can be of use to you, you need to know what they are.

The assumptions:

- You know what you want to do.
- You are intelligent.
- You can write a reasonable, straightforward sentence.
- You are motivated to create your own success.

What is **not** assumed:

- That you are a "writer" or a grammarian.
- That you have a secretary, a word processor, or even a typewriter.

This book assumes that you do not need psychoanalysis or aptitude testing; what you do need is a résumé and you need it fast. The problem with many of the books in the "get-a-job" genre is that they attempt to tell you how to discern what you want to do. The result is often a bit like swimming through quicksand, especially for the majority of us who know what it is we are after.

You may have picked up this book because a headhunter called you this afternoon, or your favorite project got canceled, or your boss yelled at you, or because you just completed your doctorate in veterinary medicine, but let us assume that what you need most is a résumé and a rational job search strategy.

My experience is that most job hunters are employed, do not have a week to read get-a-job books, and do know what their immediate objective is. If you are unsure, there are many good books on the subject. See the Appendix for a quick overview of some of the best.

You must know what you want to do next to proceed. You will not succeed if you do not.

I assume that you are intelligent. It is a fascinating statistic that in any given year, fully three quarters of Americans do not read one single book. If you are career-minded, and you are reading this book, I am going to go ahead and assume that you do not need to be beaten over the head with a concept.

Due to the brevity of this book, some very good points are made only once. It may be helpful to write in the book, take notes, or reread some parts as you go along.

Almost anybody can write a reasonable, straightforward sentence. You do not need to be a great writer, or even a good writer, to write a great résumé. Résumé writing is a formula that you are going to learn. This is business writing, not literature. Know your limitations and stay within them, and your résumé will come out fine.

Too much writing skill can actually be a detriment. One of the worst professional résumé writers I have ever witnessed wrote beautiful, vivid sentences that painted a picture just as clearly as Michelangelo, but these sentences made horrid résumés. The reader's attention was drawn to the writer's literary embellishments, not to the candidate's accomplishments.

This book does not create motivation—it channels it. My assumption that you are motivated to create your own success is a fairly safe one, because you have procured what is obviously a self-help book. On the other hand, this book is designed to make highly efficient use of your motivation.

The process of writing your own résumé can be quite exhilarating. Distilling and recounting your accomplishments is intrinsically satisfying, but the impetus to begin must come from you.

If you have read to here, pull out some paper and keep going. You will have a résumé written in no time !

Chapter 1
WHY YOU NEED A RÉSUMÉ

The résumé is an integral part of the job search process. Career books have been ringing the résumé's death knell off and on for over twenty years, but the résumé is even more popular now than ever before. I have seen good résumés for journeyman carpenters, for TV personalities, for CFOs, for management consultants, you name it. The résumé can be either a stumbling block or a springboard in anyone's job search.

In the simplest terms, here's why you need a résumé:

EVERYONE WILL ASK YOU FOR ONE.

Here's why you need it fast:

YOU ARE NOT THE ONLY ONE THEY WILL ASK.

This is particularly true of executive search consultants, also known as headhunters. Many people feel singled out when a headhunter calls them; they are convinced of the headhunter's genius and good taste. In fact, most good headhunters are on the phone all day long. They called someone else right before they called you and will call someone right after. If your lack of a résumé causes a big delay, you are out of consideration.

Another good reason to act fast is that speed creates a sense of urgency. Urgency creates momentum in the search process. Urgency and momentum make the hiring authority hire you instead of deciding to keep looking. More on this is in chapter 13, "How to Get Interviews; How to Plan and Manage a Job Search."

As you can probably tell, I am a big fan of résumés. Résumés have made great contributions to meritocracy and efficiency in American

While Eugene's competitor was away from the room, a fire broke out in his attache case.

business. We no longer live in an economy where you can just go to work at Uncle Bob's gas station or Aunt Jane's conglomerate. Even if that is still done, it is no longer the model. You sell your skills to the highest bidder, presumably the one who can utilize those skills for the greatest return. And you use your résumé to sell those skills.

Chapter 2
What Your Résumé Can Do for You

A good résumé can do four things, each distinctly separate and distinctly important:

- Get the interview
- Structure the interview
- Remind the interviewer about you
- Justify the hiring decision to others

The biggest challenge your résumé will ever face is direct competition, winning the interview in the shoulder-to-shoulder battle with other résumés, many of which are from candidates with better qualifications than yours. Some glamour industries, such as airlines, receive in excess of one thousand unsolicited résumés *per day*. Following my guidelines, my clients have often gotten interviews and jobs at odds well in excess of one thousand to one.

Writing résumés that win interviews requires an understanding of what happens to your résumé when it arrives at XYZ Corp. It is usually screened by someone whose whole purpose in life is to decide who *not* to interview. Management time is valuable, so this first screening may be done by a clerk. Even if you are applying for a $90,000-a-year job, you must make it easy for this clerk, or your application will end up alongside yesterday's newspaper in the circular file.

How to write your résumé is only one interview-winning key in this book. In chapters 13, "How to Get Interviews; How to Plan and Manage a Job Search," and 14, "Cover Letters: Don't Write One until You Read Chapter 13," I will show you how to avoid getting into that screening pile in the first place.

Everybody knows that résumés are useful for getting interviews, but not everybody realizes the résumé's other, equally important, functions: It structures the interview process, reminds the interviewer of you after you are gone, and justifies the hiring decision to others.

Most interviewers will go right down your employment history asking questions about each job. Your résumé should not tell the whole story; it should pique curiosity, begging for a clarifying question. (However, it should *not* be confusing or obtuse.)

Incidentally, you should take plenty of extra copies of your résumé to any interview. Your interviewer will often ask for one, and some interviewers ask for several as a ploy to get all of yours away from you. Then they can test your memory. Have plenty of copies and pass this test.

After the interview, the résumé reminds the interviewer of what you have to offer. Even professional interviewers are strongly swayed by your written presentation. Research has shown that after you are gone, the résumé can overwhelm the interviewer's memory of you in person. A candidate with a good written presentation will be remembered as articulate, well groomed, and intelligent; one with a poor written presentation will be remembered as unkempt, inarticulate, and ill prepared, *regardless of how the candidates actually performed in the interview.* Few candidates realize how important this résumé function is.

The one major exception to the above occurs when an interviewer decides you are lying or grossly exaggerating. In this case all credibility is lost and your written presentation is discounted entirely. See the next chapter, "The Rules of Résumé Writing."

(If you interview people, be sure to prepare the same questions for every candidate, and score each candidate's professionalism and preparedness immediately after she leaves the room. Then later, make yourself believe those scores.)

———•———

Finally, your résumé can justify the hiring decision to others. The hiring cycle is getting longer and longer. More people are involved, and everyone is afraid to make a mistake. If you are the wrong hire, it can be very difficult to get rid of you. There are people higher up in the organization who rubber stamp your hire decision without ever meeting you. The better you look on paper, the more comfortable they are. Here the wrong résumé can undo every right thing about you.

Time after time candidates have come into my office and said something like, "I don't need anything special, I've already got the job." My first thought is: Then why are they asking you for a résumé? Somebody is not yet fully satisfied, and that résumé better live up to the rest of your presentation, or the whole thing could unravel.

As you are writing your résumé, keep in mind what you want it to do for you. If you understand what your goals are, what you want your résumé to accomplish, you will do a better job of achieving those goals.

Reprinted with permission

Chapter 3
The Rules of Résumé Writing

The rules of résumé writing are simple:

- There are no rules that cannot be broken, with cause.
- Be careful of what you want, you may get it.
- Do *not* hold back.
- Do *not* tell a lie.

RULE # 1

There are no absolutes in résumé writing. In other words, every rule you have ever heard about résumés can be broken if you have a compelling reason.

RULE # 2

Be careful of what you want, you may get it. This ancient Chinese proverb is as valid today as ever. Think about what you really want. More money, more power, and more responsibility are not always as much fun as you think, especially with the wrong company.

RULE # 3

Do not hold back. This is one of the few times in your life when blowing your own horn is *exactly* what you are supposed to do. If you are timid, force yourself to think of how your spouse or best friend might describe your skills and accomplishments.

If you state your skills and accomplishments well and accurately, you will increase your chances of getting a job that will maximize your potential. This is good for you, and it is good for society. So don't hold back.

RULE # 4

Do not, I repeat, DO NOT tell a lie. A blatant lie on your résumé is the biggest mistake you can make. Besides, it reveals a lack of creativity. The "problem" you feel compelled to lie about can be solved another way. Headhunters and companies check the basic facts on résumés, and there are even consulting firms whose sole job it is to do this. If you still are not convinced, consider the following.

I had a mid-level candidate who lied to me about a college degree, which I then put in his résumé. He had a great interview with the CEO. He had a great interview with the president. He thought he had the job. The president and the CEO agreed. They decided on $90,000 for a first-year compensation package. He went to the director of human resources to fill out the papers and she said, "You know, I called your college and they have no record of you." The irony here is that neither the president nor the CEO was a college graduate. No one will hire a liar.

Then, I had a candidate who lied brazenly on her application, claiming a technical skill she did not have. To her credit, she learned the skill on her own in the first few weeks of work. *Seventeen years later,* she got friendly with a coworker and bragged of her feat. You can guess the rest of the story. She got into a fight with her friend, and the friend went to top management. She was summarily fired. Ironclad company policy. No one will retain a liar.

A lie can come back to haunt you for years and years and years. Even if it gets you hired, it is not worth it.

———————◆———————

There are no other rules. It is absolutely *not* true that your résumé must be one page. Your résumé is first and foremost a business document. It should be long enough to establish what you have to offer and short enough to entice the reader to want to know more. It should not be more than two pages without a good reason (and there are many). It should have big enough print to be easily read. It should include roughly ten years of experience unless more or less is to your benefit. All the important points should be introduced on the first page if it is more than one page. It should be printed on white or off-white paper, unless you are in the creative end of one of the visual arts. These are all useful points, but they are far from rules.

Chapter 4
Résumé English Simplified

Write a Letter to Your Sister for a First Draft

If you write a letter to your sister about your job accomplishments, and then take out all the first person pronouns and most of the helping and being verbs, all your tenses will be correct and your letter will be a great first draft of your résumé.

Put more technically: Résumés are written in the first person. The subject of most sentences will be "I." Résumé English is the same as any other written English, but with the following removed: first person pronouns, most articles, and many of the helping verbs. (True grammarians please forgive me for leaving out the 499 clarifying points. My goals are to edify without confusing and to get on with this material.)

One more time:

- Almost always delete first person pronouns. First person pronouns are: I, we.
- For a clipped and businesslike style, it is okay to delete most articles. Articles are: the, a, an.
- Delete most helping and being verbs. Helping verbs are: have, had, may, might, etc. Being verbs are: am, is, are, was, were.

For example, here is the letter to your sister:

> I have been part of the start-up management team for Rapido Architecture. I report to the president. I serve as the CFO. I participate in all strategic business planning. I have contributed to the phenomenal success of this company, from a small entrepreneurial firm to a $12 million international company with 100 employees and four offices. I directed the start-up of a subsidiary, Rapido Real Property Interests. I found a site and created a $40 million renovation project. I conducted a feasibility study for a proposed $150 million redevelopment of 3 properties in Washington, D.C.

Take out all first person *pronouns*, and most *helping and being verbs*, and as many of the *articles* as possible:

> ~~I have been~~ part of the start-up management team for Rapido Architecture. ~~I~~ report to the president. ~~I~~ serve as the CFO. ~~I~~ participate in all strategic business planning. ~~I~~ have* contributed to the phenomenal success of this company, from ~~a~~ small entrepreneurial firm to ~~a~~ $12 million international company with 100 employees and four offices. ~~I~~ directed ~~the~~ start-up of a subsidiary, Rapido Real Property Interests. ~~I~~ found ~~a~~ site and created ~~a~~ $40 million renovation project. ~~I~~ conducted ~~a~~ feasibility study for ~~a~~ proposed $150 million redevelopment of 3 properties in Washington, D.C.

The result is a good first draft of your résumé, with a smooth and correct switch of tenses:

> Part of the start-up management team for Rapido Architecture. Report to the President. Serve as the CFO. Participate in all strategic business planning. Have contributed to the phenomenal success of this company, from small entrepreneurial firm to $12 million international company with 100 employees and four offices. Directed start-up of a subsidiary, Rapido Real Property Interests. Found site and created $40 million renovation project. Conducted feasibility study for proposed $150 million redevelopment of 3 properties in Washington, D.C.

---

*Note: I have left this helping verb as a bridge between prior present-tense duties and the next few statements in past tense.

Note that current and ongoing duties are in the present tense, and past projects and accomplishments are in the past tense. Then you will want to begin to edit your draft to spice it up:

Recruited to be part of the start-up management team for Rapido Architecture....

Use Insiders' Language

Use insiders' language. Baseball players do not normally use the term "batting practice"; they say "BP." Similarly, the "players" in the financial world would seldom say "mergers and acquisitions" inside their own offices; they discuss "M&A activities." Use of insiders' language is a critical way of identifying that you are in fact an insider.

So, contrary to what other résumé books say on this issue, I encourage you to use jargon and abbreviations. Use them judiciously, but do use them. The test is simple: If everyone on the inside will know what you mean, go ahead; if the jargon might seem foreign to those on the inside, leave it out. Do not forget that your own company's most common jargon may be unintelligible outside your office walls. *That* is the type of jargon to avoid.

Some abbreviations are pretty common in most business settings. Here are a few examples of abbreviations and jargon that I think are useable in almost any résumé. They have the benefit of being efficient, and can give your résumé a hard-driving feel: ROI, P&L, T&E, CFO, LOC or L/C, A/P, A/R, CPA, DOS and most of the 5,324 other computer abbreviations. If these are not familiar to you, then they are not insiders' language to you and you should not use them. If you know them and use them in a normal business setting, then feel free to put them in your résumé.

Finally, if you are a design engineer appointed to the Space Suit Topographical Reconnaissance Inquiry Panel (SSTRIP), define it one time and thereafter call it SSTRIP.

"Strange how all six of your previous employers left the 'C' out of the word 'excellent.'"

Third Person Résumé

There is such a thing as a résumé in the third person. Sentences will read something like this: "Candidate possesses the highest standards of professional integrity . . ." Headhunters popularized this style in writing about their clients, but I feel it is stilted at best. It is, however, a very good way to write a consultant's résumé. See chapter 12, "Special Styles, More Tricks."

To sum up: Tenses should be accurate, and you should be the subject of most sentences. **Write the first draft of your résumé as though it were a letter to your sister.** Avoid complex sentence constructions. If you follow these guidelines, your English will be fine.

Chapter 5
WRITING YOUR RÉSUMÉ: STYLE OVERVIEW

The Two Major Styles of Résumé: Chronological & Functional

Although there are hundreds of variations in résumé styles, there are two major and fairly incompatible families of résumé: the chronological and the functional. In short, the chronological states experience, jobs, and dates together, usually in reverse chronological order. The functional lumps skills or accomplishments together under headings such as "Management" or "Fundraising," then lists all the positions and employers at the bottom, with or without dates.

The first person to develop and use a functional résumé was undoubtedly a résumé genius. It is absolutely the most effective style for managing an unorthodox career, a complex work history, and other résumé "problems." However, anybody with a logical or coherent work history should use some version of the chronological style. There are two very good reasons for this: functional résumés are difficult to write, and many employers hate them.

Why would an employer hate a résumé style? Because it is too good at hiding candidates' weaknesses. Consequently, candidates with problems gravitate to this style. Any experienced interviewer has wasted time interviewing unqualified applicants with intentionally deceptive functional résumés.

For example, under the "Management" heading a functional résumé may say:

> Supervised a staff of 12. Gave daily assignments and monitored quality of work performance. Planned and executed comprehensive marketing campaigns.

Then under employment it may list:

V.P., Marketing, XYZ Software Development Corp.

But when it comes time to interview the candidate for head of a corporate marketing department, the interviewer discovers that the "staff of 12" were all paperboys and papergirls, and the candidate was fourteen years old at the time; and XYZ Software Corp. was a Silicon Valley pipe dream from 1981, staff of two (i.e., this candidate and, of course, the president of XYZ). This is what can happen when accomplishments are divorced from positions and employers.

"It's just about the cutest, cleverest resume I've ever seen, but the job's not about cute and clever."

From your own point of view as a résumé writer, functional résumés are difficult to get "just right"; it takes a wordsmith to excel in this style. I personally have the highest regard for the functional résumé, and we do write them occasionally in my office, but you are better off if you can sell yourself successfully with a chronological résumé.

The bulk of my background is with a fast-track management clientele, and they usually do have coherent backgrounds. This book concentrates on variations of the chronological style that are common, conservative, and successful for my clients. If you feel you would prefer the functional style, and some qualified people do in spite of the above, then I suggest you read *The Damn Good Resume Guide,* by Yana Parker. It provides an excellent, well-written delineation of how to put one together.

Control Your Reader's Eye

Your résumé is a design project as well as a writing project. The words have to look good together, regardless of what they say. As you write your résumé, you must also design it. It should look good at arm's length, and it should **control your reader's eye.** To accomplish this, use emphasis judiciously. Emphasizers that can help you control the reader's eye are bold type, italics, underlining, font size, and capitalization. The cheapest electronic typewriters have all of these, but it wouldn't matter if you used a drafting pen to get the effect. Note: Do not mix too many different emphasizers on a page, as the result can be dizzying. Here is a sample table of descending emphasis:

Pretty Big Bold Upper & Lower Case

<u>BOLD ALL CAPS UNDERLINED</u>

<u>Upper & Lower Case Bold Underlined</u>

<u>REGULAR ALL CAPS UNDERLINED</u>

REGULAR ALL CAPS

Upper & Lower Case Bold

Extra Capitalization of Major Words with Upper and Lower Case Letters

Regular capitalization and lower case letters

Italics, only for book titles, foreign words, and very special cases.

When I want to control the eye of the reader, I will use emphasis out of the expected order. Note the following:

The University of Arkansas, Fayetteville, Arkansas
B.S., Chemistry, 1985

The reader's eye skips the school and concentrates on the degree and major. Compare with this:

STANFORD UNIVERSITY, Stanford, California
B.A., Art History, 1985

See how different these two listings are? Although in many ways identical, the emphasizers control what the reader reads, and its impact on her. Here are two more samples, just for fun:

New York University, New York, New York
B.S. Candidate, **Business Administration,** ongoing

International Business, The Wharton School of Business, 1983
University of Pennsylvania, Philadelphia

Emphasizers are so effective that most readers will read that the listing immediately above represents a college degree, especially on a screening read and especially if just one calendar year is listed. This is *not* a lie, just good résumé design.

Be aware of the balance of the material on your page, and how it looks at arm's length. This is determined by word groupings, or listings, and the space between them. The mind loves a list of three, likes a list of two, and is not too happy with a list of more than four. You can be sure that no reader is going to be eager to read a résumé without sufficient white space.

This is a pretty listing:

- Nec mora, cum omnibus illis cibariis uasculis raptim remotis.
- Laciniis cunctis suis renundata crinibusque dissolutis ad.
- Hilarem lasciuiam in speciem Veneris, quae marinos.
- Fluctus subit, pulchre reformata, paulisper.

This is a pretty listing:

- Etiam glabellum feminal rosea palmula potius obumbrans de industria quam tegens uerecundia: proeliare, inquit, et fortiter.
- Proeliare, nec enim tibi cedam nec terga uortam; comminus in aspectum si uir es, derige et grassare nauiter et occide moriturus.

But very few readers will want to wade through a block of text more than five lines deep:

Hodierna pugna non habet missionem. Haec simul dicens inscenso grabattulo super me sessim residens ac crebra subsiliens lubricisque gestibus mobilem spinam quatiens pendulae Veneris fructu me satiauit, usque dum lassis animis et marcidis artibus defatigati simul ambo corruimus inter mutuos amplexus animas hanhelantes. His et huius modi conluctationibus ad confinia lucis usque peruigiles egimus poculis interdum lassitudinem refouentes et libidinem incitantes et uoluptatem integrantes. Ad cuius noctis exemplar similes adstruximus alias plusculas, ad infinitum.

As a general rule, avoid the style of using a bullet for *every single sentence* in the résumé. I call this the Teflon™ résumé: It reads fast but nothing sticks in the mind. Also, I am definitely not a fan of the recently popular style of putting headings in the middle of the page. You read from left to right, so put your headings on the left margin.

Again, while you write your résumé, design it as you go along. It is much more difficult to fix the design than it is to do it right the first time. And be very careful to be consistent! Your design makes a statement about you as a potential employee, about your detail skills, about your marketing sense, and about your ability to do a simple assignment.

Control your reader's eye. Balance the look of your résumé on the page.

Chapter 6
Writing Your Résumé:
The One Thing You MUST Do First

You've indicated here that you would be uncomfortable accepting employment that might interfere with your nails.

Reprinted by permission of Gail Machlis

Point of View: Who is This Thing For, Anyway?

Every employer has a sentence stenciled on the inside of her eyelids: "What can this candidate do for me?" Every time she blinks her eyes, she sees this sentence. It is a question you had better answer.

This is "point of view." *Her* point of view, and the one you are going to think about as you write and design your résumé. A résumé is not a summary of your life, a chance to list accomplishments important to you, or a representation of your social and political values. It is an attempt to answer that question on the inside of the employer's eyelids: "What can this candidate do for me?"

As you write, you are going to adopt your employer's point of view. You are going to anticipate her concerns, guess what would excite her, and envision her motivations. You are going to get inside her head and sit.

Children cannot do this, cannot get outside of their own egos, but you can. You are an adult. You can foresee this employer reading your résumé. You can feel the paper, you can see her read, and you can feel her think. *You can adopt her point of view.*

I am going to ask you to adopt a point of view outside of yourself several times. Take it very seriously. It is the key to good writing of any kind, and it is the key to **great** résumés.

The One Thing You MUST Do First

The one thing you must do first is *envision the ideal candidate.* Forget about yourself entirely. Sit down, take out a fresh sheet of paper, and write down what you envision about the ideal candidate for the job you want. This is one of the most important techniques you will learn in this book. If you will do this now, the rest of your project will flow like water down the mountain.

What **features, attributes, traits, skills,** and **strengths** do you envision in this ideal candidate? Close your eyes and "see" this ideal candidate at work. See her plan and execute. See her accomplish. See her win. See her make her company happy. As you do this, write down what you see immediately as it occurs to you.

As an exercise, let us do this for two positions: a sales representative and an accounting manager. Both positions are open at Acme Widgets, a small manufacturing company with fifty-eight employees and just under $10 million in sales.

Sales Representative. The first thing I see is a smile, and it is a real smile, not a fake one. So, let's write, "friendly and outgoing personality." A related skill that comes to mind would be "never forgets a name or a face." Next, I see this sales rep working alone, so I might jot down, "able to work alone." Right away I think of "able to plan and execute a sales campaign independently," "able to develop a winning sales presentation from scratch." And I think of related administrative tasks that fall on those of us who work alone, so I write, "able to organize, track, and control a heavy work flow," and "strong follow-through on details."

Reprinted by permission of Chronicle Features, San Francisco, California.

Then, I see this sales rep trying to crack a new account, and I think how hard it is to penetrate the screen around top executives, so I might write, "able to access the top management of targeted companies." Then, I start to think of how sophisticated the sale is to this level of client, and I see a sales rep who is smart and analytical, who "can develop sophisticated cost-benefit analyses showing the bottom-line advantages of Acme Widgets."

Suddenly it occurs to me that I do not want to risk my new line of Wowie!™ Widgets on a newcomer to sales, so I want somebody with a "proven track record of success" or "demonstrated talent at opening new territories and launching new products." And I want repeat sales, too, so I write, "history of very high rates for repeat and referral business."

I am having a lot of fun with this hypothetical sales rep—we are sitting at a conference table adding up fat profits for the last quarter—when I suddenly start to think of things that could go wrong. Maybe this super-talented sales rep starts to look like an ego problem to me, so I jot down, "outstanding references from all former employers" and "ability to fit into an organization and be productive immediately," which are different ways of saying that this rep is a "team player."

Finally, in addition to gross sales, I want organizational contributions from this sales rep. I want someone who "can train new sales representatives" and "can build new dealer/distributor networks" for Acme.

Accounting Manager. Again, close your eyes and see this ideal accounting manager. My own accounting manager is so trustworthy I let her run my business, so the first things I will write are "trustworthy" and "able to meet management objectives without direct supervision." Then I think in rapid succession, "knows popular accounting and spreadsheet software," "able to learn and implement new software from documentation alone," "able to design new statements, reports, and operating procedures as needed," and "able to plan and control work flow in a deadline environment."

Just to be sure we don't miss some technical skill, let's make a laundry list of talent for our ideal candidate: "general ledger, accounts payable, accounts receivable, payroll, multistate payroll, commission accounting, cost accounting, fixed-asset accounting, cash report, quarterly and year-end report, annual profit-and-loss report, balance sheet, you name it."

Since Acme is a small business, this accounting manager is also most likely the de facto chief financial officer. So the ideal accounting manager would be "able to serve as the company representative to banks, C.P.A.s, the IRS, and vendors." Acme is probably run by a technician/founder, someone who is a good engineer and strategic decision maker, but who doesn't want to get bogged down in the details of business administration. So Acme would benefit from an accounting manager who could "support strategic decision–making through timely access to financial and other data."

Finally, since we are dealing with the *ideal* candidate, I will even write, "never makes a mistake."

Take the time now to envision the ideal candidate for your next position. Again, *this has nothing to do with you.* Have an open mind, see the candidate in action, think the ideal candidate's thoughts, take the employer's point of view, and make a big list of **features, attributes, traits, skills,** and **strengths**.

Do not read further until you have done this. When you are satisfied that you have done your best, only then should you set aside your notes and turn to the next page.

Calvin and Hobbes © Copyright 1990 Universal Press Syndicate. Reprinted with permission. All rights reserved.

Chapter 7
Writing Your Résumé:
Getting Started with the Heading

What You Need to Get Started

A pen and some paper. That's it.

If you have a typewriter, put the paper in it. If you have a computer, turn it on. Let's go. Do each section in order as specified in the following pages. If you are printing or working with a typewriter, some scissors and tape or glue would be handy, so you can literally construct the résumé when we are through.

Unless you have an emergency and simply do not have time, plan on having your finished résumé word processed. Look in the yellow pages under Résumé Service, Word Processing Service, and Secretarial Service, or ask your local copy centers about in-house word processing (many have it). Choose a place that will store your résumé for free, or give it to you on a disk. This allows for flexibility and updating as you go along.

Word processing is the standard at all levels. The quality of copiers and word processors is so high that the old prejudice against them is gone, and the new prejudice runs against offset printing as pretentious at best, and mass-produced at worst. A typeset and offset-printed résumé leads the employer to think you have printed up thousands of résumés and are applying to every company in the telephone book.

Laser printing your word processed résumé is preferred, but do the best you can within your time and money constraints. A handwritten résumé will get you the job if it is very neat, and there is a good reason for it to have been handwritten. A typewritten résumé, likewise. Do not put any more obstacles in your way. Let's write your résumé now.

The Heading

Some may think this is a ridiculously obvious part of the résumé, but I do have a few significant points about it that seem to interest people when I lecture.

You need to start with your name, address, and a contact phone number. A nickname or other name you are universally known by is okay on a résumé. If you have a really awkward first name, consider using an abbreviated form, a nickname, or your initials with your surname.

You absolutely must have a viable telephone number. Very few employers will ever write to you, except to send a courtesy "No thanks." The employer will call, most often during the day. Usually they will call several other people as well. They will not keep calling *you* back if there is no answer, if your phone is busy all the time, or if your roommate or your teenagers forget to write down your messages. It goes without saying that a cute tape machine recording is out, and should be replaced by a more businesslike message giving your first and last name, at least. In my personal opinion, no one is seriously looking for a job who does not have a functioning tape machine on his home telephone. If you do not, consider buying one today.

If any of this presents a problem, hire an answering service for the duration of your job search. Make sure they are polite and efficient, too, because many are not. Highly competitive rates are available now, and the fee will be more than worth it for the right call.

Put your office phone number on your résumé if you can. That is a judgment call for you to make. The risk is that your current employer will discover you are looking for another position. Also, if you are leaving, or at risk of leaving, your office phone may be obsolete long before your résumé is. The advantage is that other companies can reach you at their convenience during the business day.

If your employer finds out you are looking, do not be ashamed of it. It is your right in the modern world. Ever since the mass restructurings of the '80s, the covenant between employer and employee has fundamentally changed. You may even wish to sit down with your boss and engineer your own departure. On the other hand, if you do not think your company is so progressive, do not tell even your closest confidant about your considered departure. No news travels faster, not even that of an office affair.

Mr. Gregory facilitates Bob's search
for greater opportunity.

Reprinted with special permission of Cowles Syndicate, Inc.

In addition to your office phone, you may wish to list one or more of the following: fax line, voicemail, direct line to your desk, message number, or the like. If you are looking nationally or internationally, consider writing "24 hours" next to the number. Remember, the easier it is to contact you, the more likely it is you will be contacted.

Your address is not so important, except that it be understandable. Use a hyphen between a numbered street and a house number: 2201 - 16th Street. Do not use a post office box; it makes you look transient and unstable.

If for any reason you do not like your address, rent a box service. These are inexpensive, and give you what looks like an exclusive apartment address, such as 1400 Broadway, #212.

If you are serious about applying for jobs in another city, here is a very good tip: Look like a local. Use a friend's or relative's phone and address, or rent an answering service and a box service. Your local presence shows you are serious, and the employer will give you the same consideration as the other fine candidates available locally. At the middle management level and under, this technique has proved to be the clincher for my clients again and again. Do not worry if your job shows you to be three thousand miles away. It gives interviewers something to ask you right away. Warning: Relatives can be notoriously unreliable. Send yourself some mail and have a friend leave some messages, to test your communication channels.

Finally, now that you have spent so much attention on getting your heading just the way you want it, draw a line from margin to margin underneath it. That will control the reader's eye, and she will not even read it. A name and address by itself never got anyone a job, and you want your precious few seconds of screening to focus on what you have to offer.

Samples:

Marion Morrison

Local Telephone Number: (213) 555-6789

1115 - 6th Avenue South, #44   Office: (701) 555-4400
Devils Lake, North Dakota 58301   Residence: (701) 555-1209

PROFILE

[Résumé starts here. Reader starts here.]

D. Bradford Warren

24-Hour Private Voicemail: (215) 555-5661
Office: (215) 555-3211, ext. 20   231 Founding Fathers Lane
Residence: (215) 555-6551   Philadelphia, Pennsylvania 19103

AREAS OF KNOWLEDGE:

[Résumé starts here. Reader starts here.]

Kenneth J. Wilson

LOCAL ADDRESS: *MAILING ADDRESS:*
1234 Ala Amoamo Street   1234 Parker Avenue, #2
Honolulu, Hawaii 96819   San Diego, California 92182
Days: (808) 555-5242   Days: (808) 555-5242
Eves: (808) 555-5242   Eves: (619) 555-4714

PROFILE

[Résumé starts here. Reader starts here.]

Dion Vandenbosch*

Voortseweg 16
Eersel, N-B, 2248 J.D.
The Netherlands

24-Hour Message Telephone: 01131 - 4507 - 42345
Telephone: 01131 - 4507 - 43956
24-Hour Fax #: 01131 - 4507 - 34507

PROFESSION

[Résumé starts here. Reader starts here.]

Use any heading style you like. You have your paper and pen out, or your typewriter, or your word processor. Design your heading now.

Note: Dutch name, Dion Van Den Bosch, telescoped to Dion Vandenbosch to keep from confusing American employers who might not even know how to file this name.

Chapter 8
Writing Your Résumé:
Win or Lose In the First Ten Lines

The hottest résumé style on the market today is the profile style. It is what fast-track heavy hitters have been using for years to blow the competition out of the water. When it is done right, it is a beautiful, flawless device; it is the perfect marriage of form and content. Most important of all, it is so effective it is scary.

Why does it work so well? Because it answers that all-important question—"What can this candidate do for me?"—in the first ten lines. Then it goes on to let the reader know that the candidate is genuine, not a faker, in the rest of the document.

The perfect career résumé has these three distinct parts: the heading, which you just wrote; the profile of what the candidate has to offer; and the chronological career history, both work and education, which is the proof that the profile is true. The profile works only because the proof is right below it. The profile and the chronological sections are a one-two knockout punch. In advertising parlance, you have the sizzle and the steak all in one place.

When you answer the all-important question in the first ten lines, you are doing everybody a very big favor:

- Your résumé will be sorted into the "yes" pile *without even being read.*
- Your résumé will be routed to the hiring authority *without even being read.*
- Whenever it is read, it will be reviewed with sincere interest *right from the top.*

Obviously, this saves everybody a lot of time; you are capitalizing on the fact that screeners take only seconds to screen résumés. You have actually made an asset out of the biggest problem most other résumés face.

The Profile of a Winner

It is common knowledge that your résumé is an advertisement for you. In advertising, the profile is what is known as the "hook," the lines at the top of an advertisement that get you to read the copy underneath. There are car ads in national magazines with as many as five hundred words in them, about the same number as in a two-page executive résumé. All these ads have a hook at the top, e.g., "WOULD YOU DO THIS TO YOUR KIDS?" Otherwise, no one would ever read those five hundred words. It is the same with your résumé.

The names for a profile section may vary, but your heading could be any of the following:

- **PROFILE**
- **INTERESTS**
- **STRENGTHS**
- **AREAS OF SKILL & KNOWLEDGE**

So how do you write this magic bullet? Simple. **First,** make a subheading that describes your functional area of expertise, such as: "Secretary/Administrative Assistant/Executive Assistant" or "Sales/Marketing/Account Management." You can use a title, "Accounting Manager," but a functional subheading such as "Accounting" will give you more latitude. If you have divergent interests, you must choose which to feature in this résumé (you can cover the others in later versions). You have your paper out, or your computer on, so write your profile heading now. Do not worry about doing this perfectly; you can always change it later.

Second, once you have selected your heading, answer the $64,000 question in the employer's mind, "What can this candidate do for me?" Go back to your notes on the ideal candidate, circle the skills and attributes that you actually have, and make them into a little paragraph. Remember, you are the subject of each sentence: "I am able to . . ." "I have nine years of experience at . . ." "I have a solid grasp of . . ."

Do not claim skills that you do not have. If you cannot find the pencil you were just using, *please* do not claim you are "well organized and systematic." If you cannot balance your own checkbook, *please* do not claim to be "good with figures." If you are terrified to deal with strangers, *please* do not claim you have a "strong sales aptitude" or a "friendly, outgoing personality." The time you waste will not only be your own.

Remember, you are answering the question "What can this candidate do for me?" directly. You are listing **features, attributes, traits, skills,** and **strengths**. You may choose to include accomplishments or experience, but remember that experience alone is not what the employer wants to buy; he wants to buy the skills that should come with that experience. And keep it short, less than ten lines.

Use every opportunity to slant your résumé to your future. You can write a profile that begins "Interest: Real Estate Sales" even if all your sales background is in "career dresses"—or vice versa. Be sure to differentiate *ability* from *experience*. "I have the ability to run a marathon" is a totally different statement than "I have experience running a marathon." (This is a full-fledged résumé trick; do not use it unless you can follow through on your claim.)

Note that this heading and skills *profile* entirely replaces the old notion of an *objective*. You are offering your expertise, not acting as a supplicant for a position. My favorite résumé sin is an objective like the following: "Seeking a challenging and rewarding position with a progressive company with opportunity for professional growth and advancement." What does that mean, anyway? Not only is it vacuous, it is permeated with the wrong point of view. "Challenging and rewarding" for whom? "Progressive" according to whom? "Professional advancement" for whom?

One last thought: Do not be tempted to use the term "entry level" in your heading, or anywhere else on your résumé. It is the wrong point of view. It may be entry level to you, but to the hiring manager it is just another position that needs to be filled. Remember, at all levels you have skills to sell that the hiring manager wants to buy. Sell your skills; do not beg for a job.

———————◆———————

Write the rest of your profile now, drawing from your notes on the ideal candidate. To help you get started, I have pulled a few profiles as samples. Do not read ahead in the book. Finish your first draft of your profile now. Your goal is to get every major point into your profile that you want to convey to your potential employer, **but do not try to do this perfectly the first time!** Just draft a short paragraph, try to get all your ideas out, and come back to it after you have written the rest of your résumé.

Samples:

PROFILE:

Registered Dental Hygienist

> Stable and reliable, three years with current doctor, five years with prior doctor. Professional orientation is toward preventive treatment, periodontal maintenance, and patient education. Friendly, good with patients. Also experienced in office administration duties.
>
> Excellent recommendations from all doctors.

EXPERTISE:

Real Estate Acquisition, Planning, Development

Strengths include cash-flow projections, valuation forecasting, and financial and economic analysis of real estate development projects and investment assets, as well as presentations, negotiations, management, and oversight. Advanced skill with retail developments. Experience with both residential and commercial projects in the $10 million to $150 million range.

EXPERTISE:

Sales of Floor Coverings (wholesale and to-the-trade)

- 16 years in soft goods/4 years in hard goods.
- 20 years of representation to architects and designers.
- Background includes high-tech/commercial/industrial applications.
- **Proven performer** with **sales records** on behalf of every employer.

PROFESSION:

Consultant to the Mortgage Banking Industry

STRENGTHS:

- **Systems & Operations Conversions & Mergers.**
- **Reconstruction of Records, Loan Transactions & Histories.**
- **Operational Reviews, Design & Placement of Quality Assurance Measures.**

PROFILE:

Clinical Psychologist, State of Louisiana, with expertise in the following areas:

- Business, Careers, EAP, Organizational Behavior
- Psychotic/Severely Disturbed
- Alcohol & Substance Abuse
- HIV & AIDS Issues
- Family & Community Services
- Testing & Diagnostics

Effective combination of business experience, clinical knowledge, and therapeutic skill. Self-directed; comfortable with significant responsibility; able to develop programs and procedures to meet objectives; able to serve as articulate representative of employing organization.

SKILLS

Office & Administrative Management

Ability to prioritize, delegate, and control administrative work flow to manage office or entire business. Skills encompass hiring, training, and supervision of support staff; design and implementation of policies and procedures; in-house accounting through trial balance; customer and public relations; liaison to banks, C.P.A.s, and vendors; and support to strategic decision-making through timely access to financial and other data.

GOAL

A position as **Flight Attendant** with a quality-oriented airline.

QUALIFICATIONS

- Professional in manner and appearance; very strong interpersonal skills; good voice, pleasant manner; strong experience in client/customer relations.
- Ability to learn quickly, follow procedures exactly, and solve problems on my own; detail-oriented personality; ability to handle a volume of simultaneous tasks.
- History of success in public contact positions; experience with customers in multi-lingual and multi-cultural environments; management experience.
- Additional languages include Italian and French (speak, read, write) and Ukrainian (basic knowledge); some understanding of most European languages.

Chapter 9.
Writing Your Résumé: Jobs and Dates

Education or Experience First?

First, we must decide whether to list your education first or your employment history first. Education is first if you have a brand name education and you want to feature it; you are a medical doctor, a scientist, or a college professor; you are an attorney with less than five years of experience; you have a recent degree; or your education is practically your only qualification. Otherwise, experience comes before education. If you choose to list education first, skip to the next chapter, "Education & Additional Data," do your education first, then come back to list experience later. Either way, with a pair of scissors and some tape you can always switch it later.

Experience

Before you even start, you must know that this section can include part-time experience, internships paid or unpaid, volunteer experience, temporary positions, and sometimes even experience you gained in a classroom setting. Those entering or reentering the job market and those seeking to engineer a career transition will find this point of tremendous benefit. Most of us have job experience, but if it will bolster your candidacy, consider including some of these other experiences as well as, or even *instead of,* your primary job experience.

The following are all possible headings for this section. Choose one and write it onto your résumé *now*. Remember, this is just the first draft.

- **EXPERIENCE**
- **EMPLOYMENT**
- **HISTORY**
- **PROFESSIONAL HISTORY**
- **EXPERIENCE HIGHLIGHTS**

Your job subheadings underneath should include name of company, city, and date. If you are terrified your current employer will find out you are seeking employment, you can disguise the name of the company by giving a descriptive title, e.g., "A Major Reinsurance Brokerage" or "An A-V Rated Law Firm." This type of fear, however, is usually not impressive to future employers. Do not include street addresses, names of supervisors, contact telephone numbers, or other extraneous data. Control your reader's eye! You do not want your reader to get bored before she even finds out what a great job you did.

Next you will list your title, *almost always in bold.* If your real title is boring or nondescriptive, use a functional title, or use both. Your business card may just say Vice President, but you could list **V.P., Sales & Marketing** or **V.P. & Division Manager** if it is both true and more descriptive. Do not get carried away with changing your title. If the interviewer decides you are lying, your interview will be over. Besides, former employers are always willing to verify your title as part of even the most conservative reference policy. To protect yourself, you may choose to list your official designation first and put your functional title in parenthesis, e.g., **Senior Laboratory Technician (Laboratory Manager)**.

You will list jobs in reverse chronological order, which means starting with your current or most recent position, and going backwards in time from there. De-emphasize the dates by putting them on the right, not the left. If seniority is your greatest asset, you are looking for work in the wrong decade.

Sample:

EXPERIENCE:

<u>Acme Widget Emporium</u>, Chicago, Illinois   1987 - Present
Account Executive (Asst. Manager)

To create a compelling résumé, your experience listings must feature **scope of authority** and **accomplishments** more than routine duties or responsibilities. Listing routine duties and responsibilities might win a support position, but to compete for a management position you had better describe some solid, specifiable accomplishments.

Take out a sheet of scrap paper and take a few notes on your current or last position. First you will map out your scope of authority, then you will list some accomplishments. After that, you can rank them and decide what you want to include on your résumé.

Scope of authority is composed of: your title, already listed; the title of the person to whom you report directly; the size of the company, product line, division in which you work, *in dollars* if possible; the size of the product line, division, budgets, or whatever you are in charge of, *in dollars* if possible; and the number of people you supervise, and their titles and functions.

Your salary is also very much a part of the scope of your job, but it is never to be listed on your résumé. (See discussions in chapters 13, "How to Get Interviews; How to Plan and Manage a Job Search," and 14, "Cover Letters," for how to respond to requests for salary history.)

Be very exact! It is a point of psychology that more people will believe an exact figure than a rounded figure. A résumé is probably one of the only places in the known universe where $9.65 million is greater than $10 million. Exactitude makes the reader feel comfortable with your skills claims and believe in your experience.

Every time you can specify a figure, you increase the verifiability of your résumé. To a seasoned résumé reader, "supervised staff" has a slippery feel. On the other hand, "supervised 3 project engineers (team leaders), 17 design and mechanical engineers, and 23 drafting and technical support personnel" gives the reader a lot of confidence in the truth of your résumé.

The old rule from secretarial school was to spell out numbers one through ten, and use Arabic numerals for 11 and over. In a résumé, however, using 2, 3, 4, and so on makes for a good, businesslike read. I prefer "$350,000" to "$350K"; "$350,000,000" is very impressive written out fully, but it is a bit pretentious if everyone in your field would have written "$350MM" or "$350 million." Use your own judgment. Incidentally, on international résumés, "US$350 million" means "350 million United States dollars," a rather important distinction.

On your scrap paper, write a description of the scope of your job *now.*

Accomplishments are everything you did right. Throw away your position description and your flowcharts, and let the reader know what you did *above and beyond* the minimum requirements. Your accomplishments section can include problems you solved, special projects, special assignments, training, travel, commendations, awards, and honors—anything that makes you special compared to all the other people ever to hold your title.

The classic formula for accomplishment is: PROBLEM ➤ SOLUTION ➤ RESULT, hopefully with a dollar value on the result. In practice, however, you can list résumé accomplishments in thousands of different forms. Think, be creative, and be brief.

Explore different ways to represent the same basic fact. Let us suppose you are writing this résumé because you just got fired. You were fired for lack of sales, because you only sold $1,000 worth of sackbuts (a type of trombone). But wait, the account executive before you was fired, too, after having sold only $500 worth. Let's face it, sackbuts are not very popular. Looks to me like you can say *in all honesty:* "Achieved 100% increase in sales for the territory, over prior sales rep."

Search for the superlative! I cannot emphasize this enough. You are the "first," "only," "most," or "best" something, I guarantee it. Be creative. Here are some superlatives:

- Top producer company-wide, out of over 100 full-time sales professionals.
- Ranked #1 sales rep in the region for Wowie!™ Widgets product line.
- First account executive in the nation to sign an order for the new Wampum!™
- Managed the fastest growing franchise in the chain.
- Merchandised the most profitable line in the company.
- Had the lowest error rate in the department.
  and so on . . .

Observe the following transitions, each better than the last:

Accomplishment:
- Traveled to Boston for client meeting.

Accomplishment:
- Traveled to Boston with senior management for client meeting.

Accomplishment:
- Selected to travel to Boston with senior management for client meeting.

Accomplishment:
- Only intern selected to travel to Boston with senior management for client meeting.

Be sure to include intangible accomplishments. I consider a tangible accomplishment one that is figure based and that can be verified rather easily, e.g., "Increased sales by 38% in first 6 months on the job." An intangible accomplishment is not figure based and is usually a little harder to verify. Here are some examples of intangible accomplishments:

- Increased staff morale and reduced turnover.
- Improved the image of the product and the company.
- Saved several "shaky" accounts and improved account loyalty.
- Contributed improvements to record-keeping systems and overall office efficiency.

In all cases, do not be boring! Be excited about yourself! Use hard-driving language! **Start every sentence with an action verb.** "Handled" is a ho-hum verb, but "orchestrated" is a vivid, thought- and image-provoking verb. Although your résumé should not read like a war novel, use evocative verbs whenever possible. I polled the staff at Résumé Righters℠ to come up with the following list of our favorite résumé verbs.

Effective Résumé Verbs:

Create	*Implement*	*Schedule*	*Install*	*Administer*	*Attain*
Design	*Revise*	*Motivate*	*Analyze*	*Oversee*	*Evaluate*
Manage	*Reorganize*	*Coordinate*	*Prepare*	*Guide*	*Streamline*
Supervise	*Troubleshoot*	*Act as liaison**	*Teach*	*Execute*	*Maximize*
Direct	*Overhaul*	*Select*	*Promote*	*Conduct*	*Facilitate*
Establish	*Resolve*	*Compile*	*Increase*	*Provide*	*Contribute*
Plan	*Initiate*	*Produce*	*Test*	*Generate*	*Consolidate*
Devise	*Originate*	*Ensure***	*Start*	*Advise*	*Utilize*
Organize	*Train*	*Reconcile*	*Orchestrate*	*Develop*	*Negotiate*

*"Liaise" as a verb did finally make some dictionaries, but it is an odious back-formation from the noun "liaison," and I just cannot force myself to use it.

**More exact than "insure."

There is no magic to any of these. You should use words you are comfortable with, but if you get stuck just browse through this list. Sentence structures you should avoid, however, are "responsible for . . ." and "duties included . . ." These structures can almost always be replaced by more active and dynamic statements.

On your scrap paper, write up your accomplishments *now*. Be sure to quantify wherever possible, and be sure to include intangible accomplishments when pertinent. Start each sentence with a verb, and use hard-driving language.

Do not read further until you have at least written up the accomplishments of your current or last position.

Putting Scope & Accomplishments Together into Job Listings

Now you have all the components of a job listing: the company, your title, the scope of your job, and your accomplishments. Each job listing on your résumé should stack these components according to this formula:

COMPANY

TITLE

SCOPE

ACCOMPLISHMENTS

As you construct your job listings onto the draft of your résumé, you must decide what to include from your raw notes. This process also has a formula: Throw out the obvious, then rank the rest in order of appeal to your reader.

Remember your reader? Close your eyes and see that reader, someone able to give you the job you want. See that sentence on the inside of her eyelids, "What can this candidate do for me?" See her reading your list of points for scope. See what she will view as obvious and skip it. See what she will be most impressed by, or interested in, and feature each point in order of greatest impact.

Do the same for your accomplishments.

Obviously, the order in which you put things is up to you. You are not bound by the FDA to list your ingredients by order of weight or volume. If you spent 10 percent of your time answering the phones in your last office job and you are applying for a job as a receptionist, you had better list phones first and go on to typing and filing later. The "ingredients rule" for résumés is to list them in order of desired impact on your reader.

Repeat this ranking and selecting process for all relevant jobs, or roughly ten years of work history. Remember to pay attention to design as you transfer this information onto your rough draft. **You are well on your way to a dynamic résumé.**

To assist you, here are a few sample experience listings from our clients' résumés. Your listings do not need to be as long as these to be effective, but do not make them so short they do not stick in the mind.

Samples:

Amalgamated Federated Bank, N.P. & S.A., New York, New York   1978-1990
Manager, Wholesale Receivables   1988-1990

Directed billing and collections for $100,000,000 in corporate fee receivables from the bank's largest clients (all Fortune 500). Staff of six.

- Developed QA program to track productivity individually and department-wide. Successfully reduced staff by 50% with concurrent increase in productivity overall.
- Recovered $243,000 in unbilled fees in internal audit; created database and new operating procedures to prevent future underbilling problems.
- Designed Lotus 1-2-3 application to track LBO fees to comply with FASB regulations.

Manager, Bank Secrecy Compliance   1985-1987

Recruited by S.V.P. to design bank-wide policies and procedures to achieve compliance with federal Bank Secrecy Act.

- Analyzed information and form flow bank-wide. Developed and implemented policies, procedures, and training programs.
- Reduced and streamlined form flow, saving $389,000 in the first year and annually thereafter.
- Reduced error rate from 78% to 2% in six-month period.
- Developed supporting research proving improvement, resulting in 87.5% reduction of multimillion-dollar fine from the IRS.

Apex, Zenith & Acme, Management Consultants, Chicago, Illinois   1986-Present
Executive Assistant to the CEO

Manage CEO's calendar, daily schedule, and extensive travel arrangements. Represent the CEO within the organization, to our 75 affiliated management consulting firms, and directly to clients. Control information flow into and out of the executive suite. Plan and coordinate meetings, conferences and other events nationwide. Solve problems as they arise. Ensure CEO has all information and resources required for maximum efficiency.

- Hand-picked for this position by the CEO. Have achieved his complete respect and trust. *Excellent recommendation available.*
- Increased flow of information between CEO, officers, and the 75 affiliates. CEO increased travel commitments *and* increased day-to-day control over this diversified company.
- Facilitated development of new five-year strategic business plan, by handling related studies and research projects promptly (completed ahead of schedule).
- Developed and implemented a "real time" commitment tracking system to record, track, and control the CEO's obligations moment-by-moment.
- Managed relationships with 75 affiliate firms so well that much of this responsibility was delegated to me directly.
- Due to increase in efficiency in CEO's offices, was able to eliminate one position through attrition resulting in savings in excess of $30,000 per annum.

Restaurant Management Systems, Inc., Detroit, Michigan   1988-Present
Unit Manager

- Manage all aspects of high-volume corporate-owned restaurant. Full P&L responsibility, reporting to the District Manager. Strong profit performance in prior units led to assignment to this major, high-volume unit. Consistently exceed objectives for gross, net, and share.
- Hire, train, motivate staff of 34. Have gained the trust and support of personnel working in a multicultural, multiracial environment. Enjoy high staff morale and lowest turnover in the district. Personally committed to production of a top-quality product in a clean, sanitary, and attractive environment.

Selected Accomplishments:

Achieved 17.52% volume increase and 15.9% profit increase in first assignment as Unit Manager. Promoted to higher volume store. Achieved 22.05% volume increase and 19.0% profit increase. Earned Top Manager Award. Earned Profit Increase Award. Earned two Volume Increase Awards. Earned two QSC Awards (quality, service, cleanliness). Earned two cash bonuses for staff recruitment. Earned two incentive trips to Hawaii. Received two courses of advanced management training. Earned Top Ten dinner with the President (top 10% nationwide).

ArtTech Applications, Boston, Massachusetts   1988-Present
(a subsidiary of Mega-Size Computer Corporation)
President

- Recruited by the CEO of Mega-Size to turn around negative revenue trend at this wholly owned subsidiary, a manufacturer of factory floor workstations. Hired aggressive and focused management team. Reorganized accounting and control. Reduced sales force by 20%; removed cap on commissions and improved incentives for outstanding performance. Stabilized cash flow by locking major customers into exclusive annualized agreements. Increased international sales by 45%; negotiated first joint ventures with both Japanese and German business partners.
- Identified $2 billion market for product in R&D stage, a painting process control system; accelerated release, achieving full commercialization in just eight months. Rewrote business plan with new product, regained lender confidence, renegotiated terms on $6.2 million in borrowing.
- Created and managed rapid growth, from $12 million to $87 million in less than three years, with jump in ROS from 4% to 16%. Currently seeking new challenges.

What to Do about Common Problems

Whenever I give a lecture, somebody always asks me some version of "What do I do with unrelated jobs?" Either make them relevant or leave them out. Use the résumé "ingredients rule" and your own creativity to demonstrate how the experience would support your next job objective.

The following listing shows a waitress's intelligence, sales skills, and business savvy:

Neptune's Sea Palace, Miami, Florida   1990 - Present
Waitress
Act as a "sales representative" for the restaurant, selling add-ons and extras to achieve one of the highest per-ticket and per-night sales averages. Prioritize and juggle dozens of simultaneous responsibilities. Have built loyal clientele of regulars in addition to tourist trade. Use computer daily.

The next listing shows how a menial job at a letter-sorting machine can be used to support a candidacy for beginning systems analyst. The résumé reader may not know what an L.S.M. is, but you can be sure that he will be favorably impressed by this job listing.

U.S.P.S. (United States Postal Service)   Nov 1987 - Feb 1990
L.S.M. Operator
Worked average of 50-60 hours per week while full-time student, demonstrating work ethic, endurance, and sustained efficiency. Comfortable with large volume of responsibility. Excellent accuracy under deadline and in fast-paced work environment.

The prior listing illustrates a very good point about résumés: Your reader does not have to understand exactly what you have written, or exactly what you have done, as long as every possible interpretation is positive. Never be vague by accident; be vague on purpose.

Another common question is "What do I do if I have no valuable work history?" Whenever this question comes up, I think of a woman who walked into my first résumé office, many years ago. She told me she had never had a job, she had never even worked, and while we were on the subject, she couldn't do anything anyway.

As I was interviewing her in preparation for some serious creative writing, I discovered that she had been the bookkeeper for her husband's business for ten years. Her husband ran a floating fish-processing factory in Alaska, a "seasonal business" she called it. How big? "About $3.5 million dollars, more or less, depending on the season. And I guess I do manage our rental properties while he's gone every year." What did that entail? "Well, I buy property, fix it up, and rent it out." It turned out she was in total charge of the properties, a $2 million portfolio back when that was a lot of property.

Your case will be different, but I think you get the point. **Think.** You are bound to have some valuable history. Remember to consider your part-time, temporary, avocational, or philanthropic experience.

If you honestly lack valuable or related experience, **get some.** Volunteer, take a class, take a lower-level position to gain exposure. Demonstrate and substantiate your interest in your career objective. I had a client who had tried unsuccessfully for over two years to get into city planning. I encouraged him to sign up for some classes. He did, and we listed on his résumé that he was an *enrollee* in a city planning program. With his new résumé, demonstrating his *intention* to take some classes, he got a job in city planning before the first class even started. To his credit, he continued the program and eventually got his master's degree.

What do you do if you are self-employed? Employers have justified fears of the self-employed. The two main fears are that you are too independent to take orders and fit into an organizational structure, and that you will learn their business and go into competition against them. Pretty scary fears, right? Do yourself a favor. Downplay self-employment as much as possible. Do not call yourself "President," call yourself "Manager." Do not call the company "Albert Bernard Chasworth, Inc.," call it "ABC, Inc." There are exceptions, of course, but a word to the wise is sufficient. Once you are in the interview, reveal all. This type of technique is valid to get into an interview, but it is a mistake to carry it too far.

What do you do with military experience? If it is recent, treat it *exactly* like any other kind of experience. Remove the military jargon, and stress the interpersonal, leadership, and organizational aspects of your experience. If it is ancient history, you may omit it or give it a quick listing with a heading of its own.

MILITARY:
Colonel (ret.), United States Marine Corps
- Navy Cross (second highest U.S. military award for heroism in combat)
- Bronze Star (2), Purple Heart (2)

For almost twenty years, military service was downplayed or omitted from résumés, but in the last few years the honor of military service has had a sort of renaissance. If you are proud of your service, or it demonstrates important job skills, then list it. If you think it is irrelevant to your current career, leave it out.

What do you do if your most important jobs fall behind unimportant or unimpressive jobs? The answer is simple: Reorder them. List your jobs out of chronological order. Keep the dates accurate, but move listings into order according to the "ingredients rule" cited earlier. You may also wish to divide your experience under two headings — RELATED EXPERIENCE and ADDITIONAL EXPERIENCE—but doing so is purely optional.

Gaps, Dates, and More Problems

What do you do about job gaps? This is really a date question. There are many good reasons for job gaps, and it is becoming more and more acceptable to have a gap somewhere in your career. My suggestion is simple: Show the gap without comment, and be prepared to explain it in an interview or telephone inquiry from the hiring authority.

Do not fill in the missing time on your résumé with some excusatory line like, "1986–1989, family obligations." Such a line does not support your candidacy in any way. Be sure you do not fall for the temptation to "adjust" dates from legitimate experience to cover gaps. Fudging on your dates is very dangerous, and the risk is simply not proportional to the gain. See Résumé Writing Rule #4, page 5.

There are several ways to obscure and de-emphasize dates, the chief of which is to list dates by year only. I am in favor of de-emphasizing dates on general principle. Dates do not of themselves demonstrate a job skill or talent.

**"This is the best I can do
for 'previous employment.'"**

What if you have not worked in over a year? This is another date question. One of my favorite techniques for this is to take a reading like "1986–1989" and let it read open-ended, "1986–," as though you meant "1986–Present." In résumés, curiosity will almost always work in your favor. Here is how it might look:

<u>Jorgensen & Daughters General Contractors</u>, 1986-
Project Manager

Another date technique is to list experience as "current" and "prior" without specifying any dates at all. Avoid listing duration, such as "two years" or "six years," where you would have put the actual dates, as this is distracting and raises far more questions than it answers.

It is okay to leave dates out entirely, but you will face some suspicion if you do. This suspicion, however, is often an easier liability to overcome than the liability revealed by the dates themselves. Some of the résumé samples in chapters 11 and 12 have omitted or purposely obfuscated the dates, all without telling a lie.

What do you do about too many jobs, too many cities, and so on? It should be obvious by now: If you have too many jobs, omit some. If every job is in a new city, omit all the cities. Look at the following two chronologies, the same work history presented in two very different ways:

Truck Driver, XYZ Industrial Plant, Louisville, Kentucky	9/90-Present
Fire Fighter, U.S. Bureau of Lumber & Mines, Wenatchee, Washington	6/90-9/90
Delivery Driver, Sno-Frost Cake & Candy, Dallas, Texas	12/89-1/90
Welder's Assistant, Firefly Offshore Oil Field Supply, Grand Isle, Louisiana	6/89-8/89
Forklift Driver, Empire Building Supply, Ithaca, New York	6/88-3/89
Bartender, Hemingway's, Key West, Florida	4/88-6/88
Tow Truck Driver, Able Towing & Road Service, Winnemucca, Nevada	12/86-1/88

What do you think of this candidate? Unreliable, a "road scholar." Now look what happens if you take an eraser to this background:

Truck Driver, XYZ Industrial Plant	1990-Present
Delivery Driver, Sno-Frost Cake & Candy	1989-1990
Forklift Driver, Empire Building Supply	1988-1989
Tow Truck Driver, Able Towing & Road Service	1986-1988

This is still quite a few jobs, but I see a definite career path and, for a driver, reasonable duration. Tell me this candidate has a clean driving record, no tickets, and no accidents in the last seven years, and I may be interested.

———————◆———————

Hopefully by now you are getting a feel for the approach to solving these problems. Do not learn a handful of tricks from this book. Learn a way of thinking. Then you can solve your own problem, no matter how unusual it may be.

Chapter 10.
Writing Your Résumé:
Education and Additional Data

If your career has progressed logically and is well represented by your experience, your education can be rather briefly stated, with or without dates.

M.B.A., Howard University, Washington, D.C.
B.S., Economics, Duke University, Durham, North Carolina

The following education listings cover most typical cases. Some are a little more creative than others, but all are common and accepted practice.

Ph.D. (ABD), Anthropology, 1990
B.S., Anthropology, *magna cum laude*, 1986
University of California, Berkeley

ABD stands for "all but dissertation." Similarly, ABT stands for "all but thesis." These are two of the handiest little abbreviations in existence today.

B.S.B.A. (Bachelor of Science in Business Administration), *ongoing*
Arizona State University, Tempe

M.D., Harvard Medical School, Boston, Massachusetts, 1982
B.A., Biology, Reed College, Portland, Oregon, 1978

B.A., Marketing, S.U.N.Y., Buffalo, expected 1993

M.S.S.W. (Master of Science Program in Social Work), *enrollee*
University of Texas, Arlington

B.A. (Bachelor of Arts in Psychology), 1988
University of Texas, Dallas

If you abandoned an advanced degree program, do not write "M.B.A. Candidate, 1978–1979." Instead, turn it into a positive statement, as in the following:

Graduate Studies in Finance, 1978-1979
Golden Gate University, San Francisco

If you have a B.A. in music history and you are now an accountant, you may wish to list your undergraduate degree without specifying a major.

B.A., Boston University, Boston, Massachusetts

If you went to school but did not graduate, do not claim a degree. Anybody can call any registrar's office in America, say "I'm calling to verify a degree," and less than sixty seconds later they will know the truth of the matter. (Incidentally, if you hire people, make it a point to check.) If you took even one college course, you can use a listing like the following:

Psychology, Tulane University, New Orleans, Louisiana

It may not work in all cases, but if you have experience and manage your job search well, you will definitely receive consideration and you will get a good job. Accept your shortcomings *whatever they may be.* Your education will only be a stumbling block if you let it be one.

If your education is truly nonexistent, then omit it. I have had only one professional candidate in my career who did not have any college education at all. Not one day in a college classroom. Not one management seminar. Nothing. He had dropped out of high school to design sound systems for Bill Graham in San Francisco, and after several career twists, he had become a process automation engineer.

So we left education off entirely. He had a very impressive two-page résumé, which was handy because whichever page the reader was on, he could assume the education was on the other. It worked. He was flown across the continent for interviews with an exciting robotics engineering firm. They even negotiated an offer before the matter finally came up. When it did come up, my candidate was ready: "All my life I have been working on cutting-edge technology, and frankly, I just couldn't take the time out to go to school to study science that was obsolete."

He got the job.

Whatever your limitations may be, accept them and go on. Get out there and sell yourself on your strengths.

After you have a good job, then really think about getting that degree. No matter how old you are, you will not get any younger, and to paraphrase Dear Abby, "How old will you be in X years if you *don't* get that degree?" Also, as people change jobs more frequently, it is a nuisance to have to run this gauntlet over and over again.

Even if you have one degree, if you are under thirty-five you had better seriously think about an advanced degree. Your case may be an exception, but I am seeing more and more careers choked off because of the lack of an M.B.A. or other advanced education. This is particularly true in the fast lane of business, but also in any lane of education, social services, science, engineering, and even such unlikely fields as the military. Not everyone wants more and more career challenges, but if you do, take a hard look at your credentials.

———————

Recent college graduates can make a big presentation out of their education section. It can include classes, honors, awards, activities, affiliations, study abroad, special projects, their golf handicap, and practically anything you can imagine. If recent education is one of your greatest qualifications for a position, feel free to feature items like these:

University of Nevada, Las Vegas, Nevada
Candidate for the **Bachelor of Science in Hotel Administration** expected May 1991

- Dean's Honors
- St. Tropez Partnership Scholarship
- Hotel Association
- Eta Sigma Delta, International Hospitality Management Honor Society
  Vice President
- Professional Convention Management Association
- Champion, Intramural Squash

One thing that you really should think twice about listing, however, is a non-academic sorority or fraternity. Unless you were president, vice president, or treasurer, you may just want to skip it. Your success on the social committee is likely to be viewed as an exercise in creative beer drinking. No matter what they told you on pledge night, these organizations are not as universally admired as you might hope. They are increasingly identified with alcohol abuse, the number one drug problem for American business.

The most compelling college-related listings will be actual classes taken. I like to use the word "coursework" so I can paraphrase class titles somewhat more freely.

B.S., Business Administration, 1984
Michigan State University

coursework included:

- Accounting I & II
- Corporate Finance
- Statistics I & II
- Sales & Sales Management
- Marketing Strategy & Planning
- Marketing Research

computer skills:

- Lotus 1-2-3
- Cobol, Basic, Pascal
- Database II
- TSO/ISPF
- Dataease
- Paradox

This technique is particularly useful for featuring classes you may have taken outside your major, if they support your career objective.

If education is one of your only qualifications for your next position, you may also choose to pull out special projects and make them listings unto themselves. Just use a heading like SPECIAL PROJECTS and go on to write them up like experience listings (see the previous chapter). People who have built computers, solved marketing problems, designed and specified the interior of a four-hundred-seat restaurant (as school projects) will be able to get a lot of mileage out of this technique.

Finally, if you have no college experience and want to list a high school diploma, even that can be spiced up:

Diploma, College Preparatory Studies, 1988
Central High School, Middletown, Ohio
- High Scores in Math & Science.
- "Athletic Scholar" Award for simultaneous Letter and Honor Roll.

In the Northeast, it is common to list prep schools on résumés, particularly in certain industries such as finance. West of the Atlantic Seaboard I would probably recommend against it. In much of the U.S., "Phillips Exeter" might sound more like a tobacco product than an elite academy.

Write your education section *now.*

Then as you proceed through the following sections, add in pertinent data or additional headings if you need to.

Professional Credentials & Licenses

Professional credentials can be cited either at the top of the résumé or with the education. Do not assume that your reader will realize you have professional credentials because of your experience.

C.P.A., State of California, since 1972

Member of the Bar, State of New York, admitted 1985

NASD Series 7 License, current

Credentials can also be listed as "pending," if you are writing your résumé after you have sat for the exam, and before the results are released.

Languages

The business world is increasingly international. If you are even remotely likely to use a language skill in your next job, list it either in your profile, or under your education, or in a heading by itself, or somewhere under an **Additional** heading at the bottom of your résumé (see below).

The following are varying claims of proficiency, in decreasing order:

LANGUAGES:

Japanese	fully bilingual/bicultural
	knowledge of Asian business protocol
German	speak, read, write, translate, interpret, including contracts,
	scientific and technical documents
Spanish	conversationally fluent
Mandarin	business proficiency
Danish	understand but cannot speak
Russian	basic

Affiliations, Community Service, Activities

As a general rule, these categories strengthen a weak candidate and weaken a strong candidate. In any case, only the most *directly related* and *candidacy-supporting* organizations should be listed.

For example, if you are interested in a position in import/export, belonging to the World Trade Club might be seen as a plus. If you are an import/export executive, unless you are an officer of the organization or a featured speaker, I would forgo the listing.

Be sure to skip organizations whose chief criterion for membership is the ability to write a check.

———

Another use for this section is to reveal your ethnic identity. If you wish to reveal that you are gay, or African-American, or Azerbaijani, here is one place to do it. There is no doubt that membership in the Azerbaijani Students Association identifies you as Azerbaijani.

I used to think that such identifications had no place on a résumé, ever, but my point of view is changing. I tried to take an organization off a gentleman's résumé because it identified him as gay. He was very clear about why he wanted it put back: "I don't care to work in an office that is homophobic."

Although I can understand this sentiment, it is still my professional opinion that any information that can play to an employer's base prejudices, for *or* against the candidate, should be avoided. Your ability to perform your duties should be the focus of your résumé, not your status as a former model, minority, or member of a particular church.

Get the interview based on your job skills, as clearly presented on your résumé. Then use your professionalism, personality, and the strength of your qualifications to overcome any unfair and irrelevant prejudices your employer may have. If you do a good job of answering the question, "What can this candidate do for me?" your potential employer is not going to care if you are a Martian.

———

In addition to avoiding unnecessary ethnic identifications, be careful of using this section to make a statement about your personality, politics, or lifestyle.

Yoga may be a life-enriching activity for you, but mentioning it may make you seem flaky to your potential employer. Your status as a deacon in a Baptist church may be a negative factor to a Jew or a devout Roman Catholic. Even your sports activities may be an unconscious turnoff to the tired, cigarette-smoking vice president who reads your résumé at 9 P.M.

These types of information have their own name in résumé jargon: "throw-out factors." They are either irrelevant or personal data that do little or nothing to advance your candidacy, yet create a great potential for your résumé to be thrown out. In business terms, the possible upside is small, the possible downside is terminal.

If you really plan to entertain clients on the links, then maybe you should mention your golf talents. However, the general rule is: Unless you plan to do it on your job, leave it out.

Hobbies

For 99.4 percent of people reading this sentence, listing hobbies on your résumé will be fluff. Once again, only the most *directly related* and *candidacy-supporting* hobbies should be listed.

In all my years of writing résumés, I can only think of one instance that exemplifies a directly related and candidacy-supporting hobby. This particular client was an electronics technician whose hobby was designing robots for amusement. Apparently, he was a real Rube Goldberg, with a house full of robots to fetch coffee, vacuum the floor, chase the kids, you name it. If your hobby is not this strongly related to your objective, I would leave it out.

Additional

You can put a grab bag heading such as this near the bottom of your résumé. This section can contain foreign-language skills, relevant travel experiences, availability, and any loose items that you feel are important to convey to a potential employer. I try to avoid needing to write a section like this, but it is common enough to have one.

There is a résumé-writing theory that says you should end your résumé with one last punch, but I do not agree with it. Your résumé should have its punch at the top, and wind down toward the end. I certainly would not wait until this section to introduce critical information. If your qualifications are weak, however, you may wish to throw a few final hooks in the end to try to stay in the "yes" pile.

Examples:

Proven performer with a desire to tackle a new challenge. Comfortable with high-end, sophisticated, and/or technical products. Available for unlimited travel as needed.

Aspiring writer with the talent and the desire to succeed on both professional and personal levels in extremely competitive environments. Self-directed, highly energetic. Completed Bachelor of Arts degree while working full-time. Contagious intellectual curiosity and enthusiasm. Committed to the pursuit of excellence in work and lifelong learning.

If you are not a native citizen, or are likely to be identified as such, I strongly recommend that you identify your status: "Resident Alien, Valid Green Card, Qualified for Employment," "U.S. Citizen since 1985," or "Canadian Citizen since 1973."

In an American business résumé, you should *never* list your height, weight, physical condition, age or date of birth, marital status, names of your kids, or similar personal data. You immediately identify yourself as a "résumé dinosaur" who has not read a résumé book since 1958. This is not funny. Your potential employer will assume that all of your marketing and management ideas are from 1958, too.

On the other hand, if you are applying for work internationally, you should know that the entire rest of the world lists date of birth and marital status, at least. (In Japan, employers want to know which grammar school you attended, so they can discern the neighborhood you grew up in, and presumably what kind of person you are.) If you send your résumé overseas, include basic personal data, but not height and weight. The following listing was designed to allow the client to use his résumé anywhere in the world:

PERSONAL:

> Available for travel and offshore assignments for the right company.
> Date of Birth: February 2, 1960.
> Citizenship: United Kingdom. Passport: United Kingdom.
> Married to U.S. Citizen. Status: U.S. Resident Alien.
> Qualified to work throughout the U.S. and Europe, without reservation.
> References and additional details provided on interview.

References

Do not list your references on your résumé, no matter who they are. References, portfolio, transcripts, writing samples, list of publications, and the like can all be offered on request.

Some of the recent résumé books are now saying you can forgo the rote "References on request." I am not ready to do so yet. Logic says that this is an obvious statement, but humans are not always logical. It is reassuring to read this statement, even if we know it, and it lets the reader know the résumé is over.

Perhaps even more important, you can use these words as a visual anchor to your design. Just as you drew a line from border to border after your heading, draw a line from border to border on the bottom of your résumé. Then center REFERENCES ON REQUEST underneath the line. The result is a very satisfying look, a well-balanced résumé.

———————◆———————

Congratulations. The first draft of your résumé is done.

Chapter 11
Writing Your Résumé: Putting It Together

Take a long look at the first draft of your résumé. How does it look? How do you feel?

Most of us find the act of putting together a résumé exhilarating, even cathartic. Seldom in life do we sit back and really take account of our accomplishments. In a thousand ways, every one of us is an unsung hero. This is one chance we have to sing that song. Take a moment to savor it.

Now look again. Think. Did you leave anything out? If you did, stop now and put it in. Do not worry about how long your résumé is; we will address that in a moment. When you are satisfied that everything that needs to be in your résumé is in it, only then will we proceed to take things out.

Final Edit

There are several techniques to shorten, strengthen, and improve your presentation. To put it simply: Throw things out or summarize them.

Ernest Hemingway called his eraser a "shit detector." Take a look at your sentences. How many adjectives can be thrown out? How many statements will be obvious to your intended reader? Check your résumé for tone. Be especially wary of sounding pompous. "Excellent" and "outstanding," when applied to yourself, can have an unintended effect on the reader.

Your résumé should wind down toward the end. As a general rule, each job listing should be a little shorter than the last. Give your recent experience full exposure, but as you get back to ten years ago and more, just stop. This has a very interesting effect. If you remove dates from your education, it is impossible to date you. You cannot be discriminated against because of your age, whatever it is, since your age is not available.

Employers have in mind a profile of the candidate they are looking for. That profile can be very specific. This is not really a form of prejudice—though it can work out that way—just standard management planning. The best managers think visually, they project the future visually, and you may not be in that vision. So revealing data that can count against you, *even subconsciously,* is something you should avoid. Once you are in the interview, you can easily demonstrate why you are the right person for the job even if you were not the candidate they had in mind. Do not let subconscious prejudices keep you from getting an interview. Keep throw-out factors out of your résumé.

Besides, few banking vice presidents are stronger candidates because of a full delineation of their duties as a "Vault Teller" early in their career. If you have older experience that you feel supports your candidacy, use an encompassing statement without dates:

PRIOR:

Executive Assistant to the CEO, Ajax & MacDonald Machine Tool Co., Akron, Ohio

Office Manager, Dewey, Cheatham & Howe, New York, New York

The same technique works under education:

ADDITIONAL:

Technical Training, Workshops & Seminars (numerous)

Now look your résumé over and see if anything is annoying to you. If it is, it is probably not true, or not you. If it is not true, take it out. If it is not you, but it is true and it will improve your candidacy, *try to leave it in.*

I know from experience that some people are not comfortable with profiles stating their skills and abilities. If everything in your profile is true, factual, and not pompous, then go with it. If you are using your résumé inside your own company, or applying to a position through a direct, guaranteed contact, then you might decide to drop your profile. (If you do drop your profile, save the wording. Often it can be included in your cover letter, sometimes verbatim.) Without the profile, your résumé is a "classical" management-style résumé. Even if you drop the profile, your résumé will be better because you wrote a profile first, and it helped focus your thoughts throughout. If you are going to face heavy, direct competition—or if you are applying to people who are in no way obligated to speak with you—then I would recommend you use the best profile you can write.

Finally, check your résumé for point of view one last time. Is everything really in the order of maximum desired impact on the reader? Take your time with this. The order of your information is second in importance only to the information itself.

Except for the grammar and spelling, do not be a perfectionist. A perfectionist will still be working on his résumé long after you have a great new job.

Production

Unless you have a computer and printer at your disposal, you will need to contract for word processing and printing services. As mentioned in chapter 7, look in the yellow pages under Résumé Service, Word Processing Service, and Secretarial Service, or call local copy centers to see if they provide word processing services.

Do not be surprised if you have to tinker with your résumé to get the design just right. Fonts and type sizes are different on different systems. You will need to verify that you like the spacing, layout, and overall design in its final form.

If you are a management-level candidate, I recommend a conservative presentation. A very simple border, at most, might be okay, but otherwise avoid fancy layouts and designs, details such as little pointing hands, and other bells and whistles. These detract from your qualifications.

Whatever you do, do not let someone talk you into some kind of fold-out or brochure format. These are ostentatious and notoriously unpopular with employers. Use standard size paper. Use white or very light grey paper if you are an executive. Others can use off-white paper of various hues, but I would think more than twice about pink or blue. White has come back in style of late, and it can be copied or faxed without loss of readability.

The weight of the paper is actually as important as the color. I recommend heavy paper, as it subconsciously denotes a candidate with substance. If you hand someone a stack of résumés, she will pick a disproportionate percentage of the ones on heavy paper.

Once you are happy with your design, either print it straight from the computer on a laser printer, or photocopy from a master on a high-quality photocopying machine. The quality of these copying machines is so high now that only a graphic artist would notice the difference between the copy and the original. Better papers will usually have a watermark, so no matter how you print the final version, be sure that the watermark on the paper is right-side up. Printing onto the paper upside down or backwards is indicative of a sloppy, inattentive candidate.

While you are printing your résumé, get some 9×12 envelopes. Your beautiful résumé should not arrive all folded up, with the print flaking off. It should arrive flat, like any quality presentation. Besides, if you have to open a stack of mail, what do you open first? I prefer white 9×12 envelopes, which are known as catalog envelopes. Do not forget, a 9×12 envelope requires extra postage, even if it is under one ounce. It would not be graceful for your résumé to arrive postage due.

———————◆———————

Your Overnight Résumé is now done. If you are not mailing your résumé and do not need a cover letter, you can skip the rest of this book. You might want to read the section entitled "Job Search Protocol," in the next chapter, however, as it applies to practically everybody. GOOD LUCK !

Additional Assistance

The following pages contain complete samples of well-designed résumés. Look them over as a guide, but do not copy any sentences verbatim. Résumé styles change and evolve, and today's hot phrase is tomorrow's cliché. (For instance, it's not progressive to use the word "progressive" anymore). The best way to make sure your résumé is fresh is by writing it yourself.

If you decide you need additional help, there are two good sources: your friends, and a résumé-writing professional.

Do not be worried or surprised if you get ten different opinions when you show your résumé to six different friends. Use the principles outlined in this book and your own good judgment to sort through their suggestions for the ones you think are valid.

If you use a résumé-writing professional, be sure to shop around. Ask to see samples, make sure the design is good, then actually read them. A good design is worthless if there are typos and errors in the work. Finally, your writer should have a good honest approach. Hype and fluff are damaging to a well qualified-candidate.

If you do not find a good writer locally, then call us here at Résumé Righters[SM] in San Francisco, (415) 543-2020. We have management and executive clients throughout the United States, and in Sydney, London, Zurich, and a few other places as well. We serve their needs by fax and by overnight courier. Our rates start at about $200, and we work on a satisfaction-guaranteed basis.

Sheryl Yen

270 Holokai Place
Honolulu, HI 96825
(808) 555-6210

PROFILE:

Skilled small business manager with technical skills in framing and art preservation, demonstrated talent for sales and customer service, and ability to hire and supervise an intelligent and motivated staff. Experience with major commercial accounts. Back office skills include administration, personnel management, and accounting/bookkeeping.

SKILLS:

- Mats, Specialty Cuts, Oval & Circle, Multiple Opening, Filets, Fabric Wraps
- Dry Mount, Spray Mount, Wet Mount
- Glass, Mirror, Plexi, Plexi Boxes
- Cut Wood and Metal Frames
- Canvas Stretching and Needlework
- Shadow Boxing
- Conservation/Preservation/Archival Framing
- Fine Art Packing/Shipping/Insurance

EXPERIENCE:

Frame Land, Honolulu, Hawaii, 1986-1990
Manager

In full charge of the main store and workshop. Reported directly to the owner. In charge of a staff of 25. Monitored inventory and served as buyer for all six stores (framing materials, fine art prints, workshop supplies, office supplies, promotional materials). Handled accounting, A/P, A/R, credit, and billing. This was a strong business, generating up to $62,000 each month from main unit alone.

Supervised shop and workshop. Provided technical expertise to all staff and retail customers. Handled specialty framing personally. Clientele was approximately 60% retail and 40% corporate and to-the-trade.

Provided V.I.P. service to interior designers, corporations, art consultants, galleries, and professional artists. Represented company to accounts. Handled entire sales/service cycle, including setting up credit accounts and billing.

Windward Community College Photography Department,
Kaneohe, Hawaii, 1984-1985
Laboratory Technician

Coordinated lab activities for 60 students. Provided technical expertise and consulting on technique. Monitored chemistry of developing agents. Maintained equipment. Ordered supplies, opened and closed the lab, ensured clean and safe environment.

EDUCATION:

B.F.A., Art, 1986
Windward Community College

RECOMMENDATIONS PROVIDED ON REQUEST

LOUISE CUNNINGHAM

1234 Peachtree Lane
Savannah, Georgia 31419

Office: (912) 555-1616
Residence: (912) 555-1328

EMPHASIS:

Real Estate Lending

Top producer. Major accomplishments in sales management and processing operations. Aggressive, entrepreneurial, systematic. Strengths: (1) providing leadership to a staff of top producers, (2) building close ties with major and minor players in the real estate community, (3) creating quality loan portfolios by originating preferred risks and through technical understanding of instruments and documentation.

EXPERIENCE:

Georgia Federal Savings & Loan, HQ: Atlanta   8/86-Present
A.V.P., District Loan Center Manager, Savannah & Albany

Selected to take over this loan center, the largest loan center outside of the Atlanta metropolitan area, fourth largest in the entire branch system. Manage $200,000,000 annual production, plan $500,000 operating budget, direct staff of 35 (Supervisors, Sales Reps, Closers, Underwriters, Processors). Includes income property, construction and residential real estate lending, especially FHA, VA, FNMA, ARM, and Jumbo instruments; all phases from origination through underwriting and funding.

Accomplishments:

- Recruited to run the most productive branch outside of Atlanta.
- Decreased turnaround time from 18 days to 7 days in first 6 months.
- Reduced audit errors to virtually nil in six months.
- Exceeded production goals every quarter.

A.V.P., District Loan Center Manager, Albany

Accomplishments:

- Achieved #1 market share with over $80,000,000 in funding per annum.
- Reduced turnaround time from 45 days to less than 15 in first six months.
- Served as interim Manager for Macon office.
- Exceeded production goals every quarter.

Security Southern National Bank, HQ: Atlanta   11/85-8/86
Manager, Real Estate Lending, Valdosta

Accomplishments:

- Recruited to launch new office, reporting to Atlanta-based V.P.
- Developed and implemented sales/marketing campaign.
- Built new business from $0 to $5,000,000 in first 6 months.
- Ranked #1 in South Georgia and #2 statewide, with a brand-new office, in less than one year.

Northeastern Savings & Loan, Regional HQ: Macon   2/84-11/85
Real Estate Account Executive, Macon

Accomplishments:

- Frequently ranked Top Producer in region, *consistently* ranked top 5% statewide, out of over 100 Account Executives.
- Also excelled in position as Financial Analyst, acting as budget and reporting liaison between four departments and senior management.

EDUCATION:

B.S., Business Administration (Finance)   1983
Brigham Young University, Provo, Utah

- Dean's Scholarship
- Spanish (speak, read, write)

Angelina Villanueva

1232 Calle Allegre del Sur
Phoenix, Arizona 85018
(602) 555-6388

STRENGTHS:

Staff & Operations Management

Demonstrated talent for management of customer service operations. Skills include staff selection, training, and motivation; conscientious application of policies, procedures, and systems for inventory and cash control; budgeting and financial control in a corporate profit-center environment; community relations and promotions; computers.

Career committed. Energetic, with proven stamina (long hours, heavy work load). Available for travel and continued relocation as needed for the right opportunity.

EXPERIENCE:

Burger Empire Corp., Phoenix, Arizona, May 1988–Present
General Manager

Full profit and loss responsibility for $1 million unit. Train, motivate, and supervise staff of 35 including Assistant Managers and Shift Managers. Took a very proactive approach and turned this unit around from an "F" rating to top ranking.

- Dramatically improved unit gross and margin by tightening operations, retraining key staff, and improving food quality and speed of delivery.
- Improved staff morale; reduced turnover to record lows. Recently certified that 95% of staff has "above standard" level of performance.
- Successfully developed future managers. Two staff members promoted to Assistant Manager and one is now General Manager of her own unit.
- Selected to serve as judge on Restaurant Manager Review Board. Also act as Assistant Market Manager and District Training Manager.
- Participated in management training series, winning recognition as Valedictorian of the PRO 2 Class.
- Selected to give presentation in company's college recruiting video.
- Earned "Best in Region" in quality competition.
- Earned "Restaurant Manager of the Year," *Number One Nationwide!*

Currently seeking greater challenges and career growth commensurate with ability.

EDUCATION:

M.B.A. Candidate, Arizona State University, ongoing
Concentrations: **Management** and **Finance**

B.S.B.A. (Bachelor of Science in Business Administration), 1988
University of Denver, School of Hotel & Restaurant Management

Architecture Major, 1983–1985
University of Oregon, School of Architecture

College Activities:
Gold Key National Honor Society
Sigma Pi Eta
Chairperson, Area Standards Board

REFERENCES ON REQUEST

KATE NICCOLLS

1472 Telegraph Avenue, #19
Berkeley, California 94706

Office: (415) 555-3115
Residence: (415) 555-2766

STRENGTHS:

Sales . . . Marketing . . . Account Relations

Senior level account manager. Direct interface with client company president and senior officers. Comfortable in highly competitive markets. Able to create client loyalty above and beyond the sales relationship. Dedicated to providing a high-quality performance for a high-quality product, service or company.

EXPERIENCE:

Gannett Outdoor
Account Executive

10/88–Present

Sell local and national outdoor advertising space to media companies, advertising agencies, and businesses with Northern California headquarters.

Set records for sales performance:

- #1 Top Producer as of first quarter 1990.
- Achieved 1990 target for annual sales in the first quarter of 1990. Consistently run 175% to 225% of company targets.
- Increased territory by 56% in first six months in position, and continued to achieve highest sales in history of this territory and highest profitability in last seven years.

Brought on board many new accounts. Samples:

- Jenny Craig, first-time Gannett advertiser. Directed Sacramento test program, generating extensive free media publicity. Earned national rollout.
- The North Face, first-time Gannett advertiser, Bay Area, Denver, and New England placements.
- KFOG, first-time Gannett advertiser, converting account from long-time relationship with major competitor.
- Volkswagen, won highly competitive bid, gaining a Gannett exclusive for local market. Worked closely with both company execs and agency account staff.

Marketing Associate

Originally hired as an account relations representative, entertaining client V.I.P.s when in the Bay Area and troubleshooting problem accounts.

- Promoted to Account Executive due to success in securing the Corona Beer outdoor campaign and due to repeated requests of clients to work with me as A.E.

Evans / S.F.
Account Executive (managed largest account, 65% of total gross billings)

1988

Grey Advertising
Assistant Account Executive (Wyse and Consolidated Freightways)
Media Planner (earned promotion to account staff)

1985–1988

EDUCATION:

Stanford University
B.A., Psychology, 1984

Also: Graduate, Media School, Media Directors Council of San Francisco

Graduate, PSS1 Learning Skills Sales Training Course

Certificate, Marketing, Foothill College

Matthew A. McMahon

1237 Lake Shore Drive, North
Chicago, Illinois 60610
(312) 555-1123

---

objective

A drafting or design development position with a licensed architectural firm, with an opportunity to utilize and refine my skills and knowledge.

skills

Technical drafting, plans, sections, interior and exterior perspectives, isometric and axonometric drawing, rendering, presentation construction documents, autocad, sketching, photography.

Coursework in HVAC, lighting design, autocad, architectural engineering, architectural history. Experience as design student in Europe.

Fluent in French (speak, read, write).

education

University of Illinois, Champaign, Illinois
◆ Bachelor of Science in Architecture, 1990
◆ Design project selected for presentation to the East St. Louis Redevelopment Committee.

L'Ecole d'Architecture et de l'Urbanisme, Versailles, France, 1987-1988
◆ Dean's List. Straight "A" grade average.
◆ Gained rich understanding of variety of architectural styles.
◆ Studied design in foreign context. Expanded understanding of other cultures.

projects

Hessel Park Christian Reform Church, Champaign

Student Residence Hall, Versailles

Museum for Theatre and Dance, Paris

Multiuse Commercial Facility and Theme Park, Discovery City

employment

Smith-Baxter Associates, Chicago, Fall 1990
◆ Worked directly with the principal on design development project.
◆ Produced measured drawings of house, cafe, and warehouse.
◆ Organized drawing library and contributed to office management.

portfolio

Portfolio, references, transcripts, and additional information provided on request.

Wade A. Stevenson

12770 Bellview Drive
San Antonio, Texas 78209

Telephone / Message:
(512) 555-5187

STRENGTHS:

- **Restoration**
- **High-End Renovation & Remodeling**
- **General Contracting:** *Residential / Commercial / Industrial*

PROFILE:

Over 25 years of experience with last 9 years as Project Manager or Super. Have pursued advanced understanding of multiple trades, especially carpentry, drywall, painting, surfacing and sealing, electrical, plumbing, tiling, and masonry.

Personally interested in working with a quality-oriented outfit.

EXPERIENCE HIGHLIGHTS:

Restoration Design & Construction, San Antonio, Texas 1982–
Project Manager and **Superintendent**

Managed true, historical restorations of high-end residential properties and some commercial strips and buildings in and around San Antonio, especially in the King William neighborhood (all 100+ year-old homes). My personal specialty was kitchen and bath designs to update these homes in the historical styles. Carried projects from concept to completion, working with client, engineers, architects, subs, and suppliers.

Sample Projects:

- Project Manager for the historical restoration of Southern Pacific Railroad Depot, including the renovation of the depot ceiling and a 16' diameter stained-glass window.
- Rebuilt to scale from old photographs a complete Alcatraz prison cell inside the Alcatraz Bar & Grill in Austin.
- Superintendent on $6 million restoration and rehab of 5000 s.f. commercial building into a mixed-use condo and retail/restaurant complex in downtown San Antonio.

Schouten Construction, Englewood, Colorado, 1976-1982
Foreman and **Lead Carpenter**

Troubleshooter for this government contractor, working to U.S. Army Corps of Engineers standards. Various short-term assignments nationwide with small crews of up to 10.

Sample Project:

- Took 6-man crew into King Salmon, Alaska, and built radar site with support buildings in 3-month building season.

EDUCATION:

Chicago Technical College, Chicago, Illinois
Blueprint Reading and **Drafting**
- Plus dozens of product seminars over the last 25 years.

Elizabeth Fleck

Telephone:
(216) 555-1165

3721 Homestead Road
Cleveland, Ohio 44121

PROFILE: Seeking a position as **Accountant/Bookkeeper** or **Administrative Assistant** with accounting/bookkeeping duties. Professional and articulate, qualified for client/customer interaction at all levels. Prefer position with challenge, diversity, and opportunity for professional advancement.

SKILLS:
- Experience with small business accounting through financial statements and P&L. Includes G/L, A/P, A/R, P/R, balance sheet, trial balance, reconciliations, preparation of tax documents, and interface with C.P.A.s.
- Computer skilled, including facilitating conversions from manual to computerized. Effective problem solver. Capable of prioritizing and managing a heavy work flow without direct supervision.
- Additional skills include general office, showroom reception, telephones, client interaction, and all administrative functions.

EXPERIENCE: **Bookkeeper**, Archadeck   (temporary) 2/91-6/91
- In full charge of P/R, A/P, A/R, financial statements, reconciliations, and trial balance for two business entities, the corporate HQ and one wholly owned franchise. Interfaced with 30 other franchise operations. Brought books from four months behind to current. Facilitated conversion from manual to computerized accounting for both businesses.

Bookkeeper, Miller Tomback Corp.   2/88-12/90
- Managed A/P, A/R, and subsidiary ledgers; prepared company P/R; prepared financials through P&L. Controlled the invoicing system from origination through posting to customer account. Computed billing and mailed statements. Formulated weekly aging reports for collection of overdue accounts. Completed cost accounting and profit calculations.

Bookkeeper, Bavarian Enterprises   9/85-1/88
- Posted to A/R and A/P journals, computed P/R, prepared P&L statement, analyzed employee sales, prepared W-2s. Brought books up from six months behind schedule to current. Developed daily checkout system that revealed shortages. Devised monthly sales analysis to compare sales-per-hour by employee.

Full-Charge Bookkeeper, Goodpasture, Inc.   8/87-1/88
- Set up all bookkeeping systems for this new business. Completed this project concurrent with above duties.

EDUCATION: **B.F.A.**, Interior Design, Virginia Commonwealth University   5/84

ADDITIONAL: Additional experience in **Sales** and in **Interior Design**. Hobby: design/build/refinish furniture. Available for overtime and business travel as needed.

REFERENCES: Good recommendations available from all former employers.

RICHARD R. GLASTON

200 East Pearson
Chicago, Illinois 60611

Office: (312) 555-4467
Residence: (312) 555-8749

PROFILE:

Sales . . . Account Management . . . Sales Management

Can plan and execute complex direct-sales programs, with emphasis on building business partnerships and generating customer loyalty. Strong background encompassing sales, distribution, marketing, merchandising, staff motivation. Comfortable with government relations and contract administration responsibilities in addition to sales.

EXPERIENCE:

Gladstone Tire & Rubber Co.   1985 - Present
Area Field Manager, Mileage Sales, Chicago

Develop and service the major transit accounts based in Chicago, Detroit, Milwaukee, and Madison. Interact with contract administrators and purchasers in municipal governments and interstate trucking firms. Plan and conduct business development campaigns. Forecast sales and budget data for territory.

Prepare formal bids and proposals, including technical presentations and cost/benefit analyses. Negotiate details of contracts and agreements. Indirectly supervise a total of 33 service technicians.

- Assigned to territory to boost sales and turn around negative share trends. Increased monthly revenue from $250,000 to $400,000, a 60% increase in revenues in a mature market!
- Contributed to engineering and product development to meet customer specifications.
- Converted accounts from competitors; increased tire leasing activity; increased market share in a highly competitive market.

Account Executive, New York City Transit Authority Account, New York

Similar to above, servicing the largest single account in the nation, a $4.8 million relationship.

- Served as liaison between polymer engineers and upper management on product performance and testing; audited all account-generated reports.
- Successfully recruited, retained, disciplined, and motivated a staff of 28 technicians, with emphasis on labor relations that successfully avoided unionization.
- Coordinated distribution, including control of inventory parts and stock shipments.

Management Trainee, Akron

Training rotations through contract administration, sales, computerized sales planning and reporting, auditing, forecasting, and personnel management.

- Hand-picked from my training class to serve the NYC Transit Account.

R.J. Reynolds Tobacco Co.   1981 - 1985
Sales & Merchandising (full-time while in college)

EDUCATION: **Accounting,** University of Akron   1981 - 1985
                  Chemical Engineering, Ohio State University   1980 - 1981

INTERESTS: Marathon Runner. Health and Sports Enthusiast.

REFERENCES ON REQUEST

Paul E. Davis

5417 Wilshire Blvd., Apt. 430
Los Angeles, California 90036

Office: (818) 555-4775
Residence: (213) 555-8629

PROFESSION

Public Relations and Corporate Communications

Strengths include account management, concept development, media interface, event planning, and account team leadership. Skillful at encapsulating issues and presenting client issues in larger industrial/economic contexts. International orientation; bilingual French/English, proficient in German. Computer skilled.

EXPERIENCE

Technaucracy Public Relations, Inc., Burbank, California, 9/87 - Present
Account Executive

Plan and implement full-scale corporate and product communications programs, including event planning, media relations, and collateral materials development. Account team of 6.

Activities:

- Conceive strategies and coordinate logistics for press conferences and national press tours.
- Schedule and monitor client product demonstrations at trade shows and press events.
- Manage ongoing client relations with key trade and business press and industry analysts.
- Coordinate development of design and copy for all promotional and collateral materials.
- Oversee client and agency relationships with designers, writers, photographers, other vendors.

Accomplishments:

- Landed client meetings with *New York Times, Wall Street Journal, Fortune, Venture, Business Week, Christian Science Monitor,* and many, many others.
- Solidified a "shaky" account by placing Division Chief's speech in 3 key publications.
- Contributed promotional strategy for rollout of 2 new products and oversaw presentation at Comdex trade show, resulting in favorable reviews by industry press and analysts.
- Discovered critical information about a client and cancelled media tour, thereby saving client's and agency's reputations.

Accounts:

- Xerox Corporation
- CADAM/Lockheed
- Kyocera Corporation
- Cipher Data Products
- Fujitsu America
- Harris Corporation

The Carmichael Group, Los Angeles, California, 8/86 - 8/87
Public Relations Intern (legal, accounting, and architectural clients)

The Oregonian, Portland, Oregon, 7/85 - 7/86
Reporter, Business Features

EDUCATION

B.A., Journalism, University of Michigan, Ann Arbor, 1985
Honors:

- Alpha Gamma Sigma (scholastic honor society)
- Alpha Mu Gamma (foreign language honor society)

Kimberly Haase

37 East 9th Street
New York, NY 10003

Office: (212) 555-3276
Residence: (212) 555-7914

STRENGTHS:

Effective communicator and interface between senior management, buying office, sales floor, vendors, and V.I.P. customers. Experienced supervisor, motivator, trainer. Good leadership ability, including setting a high standard for service. Able to coordinate and focus the efforts of others. Also: computer and analytical skills.

EDUCATION:

B.A., Social Sciences, University of Southern California, Los Angeles   1987
    Emphasis: Organizational Behavior/Industrial Psychology

University of Paris, France—Sorbonne   1986
    Studied French Language, Culture, and History

EXPERIENCE:

MACY'S, New York   1987 - Present

Assistant Buyer, Towels, Bath Shop   1989 - Present
Prepare and execute seasonal plans for $10 million in business. Analyze and report on sales and product flow. Communicate closely with 24 stores. Negotiate with vendors. Coach store sales staff. Use computer to analyze profitability and flow-through by multiple factors (style, color, size, store, etc.). Contribute to exclusive product development.

- Developed a home fragrance business that ran 100% increase. Coordinated development with vendor; personally directed store merchandising and educated sales staff on product.
- Appointed Mentor in Macy's Management Training Program.

Sales Manager, Small Electrics, Personal Electrics, Microwaves, Gadgets   1988 - 1989
Trained, developed, and motivated a staff of 19 sales associates. Ensured compliance to store policies and procedures. Set a high standard for attentive sales. Communicated closely with Buying Office. Oversaw combined sales of up to $1 million per month.

- Initiated, designed and merchandised a travel shop within the department. This concept was very successful and was expanded to all stores.
- Developed and promoted a microwave "cooking school" on Saturdays, to reduce the number of microwave returns.

Selling Supervisor, China/Crystal   1987 - 1988
Coached and managed a staff of 14. Taught sales associates how to build a clientele book. Set protocol for increased telephone contact and follow-up with customers.

- Analyzed and reorganized the selling floor for increased profit and turn.

PRIOR:

Training Assistant, John Haase & Associates, Beverly Hills, California   1986
Intern, City of Beverly Hills, Personnel Department, Beverly Hills, California   1985

REFERENCES ON REQUEST

STEPHAN DAVIES

832 Pacheco Drive, Apt. B
San Jose, California 95132

Telephone/Message:
(408) 555-9210

PROFESSION: **Mechanical Designer** and **CAD/CAM Specialist**

SKILLS:
- CAD, AUTOCAD, Computervision CAADS-4X, CALMA, and others for mechanical and electrical design (2-D, 3-D, and modeling over time).
- Solid knowledge of engineering math: Analytical Geometry, Algebra, Trig, as well as Applied Math for Physics.
- Experience in a range of Aerospace, Biomedical, Process Automation, and Production Engineering projects.
- Qualified to serve as integral member of engineering team, contributing to all stages from conceptual design to final drawings.

EXPERIENCE: **Litton Industrial Automation,** Alameda, California, 2/90-12/90
Mechanical Designer (Contract Services, Inc.)
- Design layouts and design details for mechanical assembly; detailed manufacturing drawings for fabrication.
- Solved alignment and lockdown problems related to reflective mirrors and support structure used in optical laser-beam data-verification system.

FMC Ground Systems Division, San Jose, California, 8/89-12/89
Mechanical Designer (Butler Services Group)
- Modification of mechanical parts used in hull of FAADS-LOS ground defense vehicle using Computervision CAADS-4X.

Target Therapeutics, San Jose, California, 10/89-12/89
Mechanical Designer (Contract Services, Inc.)
- Design and detail drawings of extrusion device used for fabrication of high-precision plastic catheters used for heart-vessel and brain-vessel repair.

Edible Technology, Inc., Sunnyvale, California, 5/89-8/89
Mechanical Designer/Drafter (Contract Services, Inc.)
- Mechanical drawings of operating parts for an automated pizza-vending machine.

ZETA Labs, Sunnyvale, California, 7/86-2/87
Electrical/Mechanical Design Drafter (Contract Services, Inc.)
- Layout of mechanical microwave housings, mechanical layouts, electrical schematics, wiring diagrams, and trace layouts.

Calspan Corp., NASA/AMES Research Center, Moffett Field, California
Drafting Specialist   7/85-6/86
- On-site drawings of Alperin vertical injector engine, wind tunnel modification drawings, wind tunnel pressure test probe drawings.
- Also: designed fixtures for wind tunnel calibration.

EDUCATION: **A.A., Mechanical Design Drafting,** De Anza College, Cupertino
Scientific/Technical Program, NASA/AMES Research Center
AUTOCAD Training, The Copper Connection, Inc.

ADDITIONAL: Seeking long-term, permanent position. Willing to start in contract or project capacity to prove skill and value. U.S. Citizen. Availability: Immediate.

Sharon Mason

937 Brunswick Street
New London, CT 06320
(401) 555-8110

SKILLS: **Operations Analysis**
Procedures Design & Documentation
Staff Training

TECHNICAL: **Radiological Engineering**
Environmental Engineering
Industrial Hygiene

EDUCATION: **B.S., Physics (Nuclear)**   1988
Arizona State University, Tempe, Arizona

Nuclear Physics	Optics
Electricity & Magnetism	Electromagnetic Fields
Thermal & Statistical Physics	Chemistry & Biology Core Series

Certificate, Radiological Controls for Engineers   1989
U.S. Navy

EXPERIENCE: Department of Defense, Naval Shipyard, New London, Connecticut
Nuclear Engineer   1988-Present

- Design and incorporate radiological controls into technical work documents. Write radiological control procedures into each project document based on project-specific parameters.

- Serve as Lead Engineer of Maintenance Teams. Direct the removal and decommissioning of heavily contaminated equipment.

- Develop and deliver staff training on (1) reactor plant systems, (2) quality control of operations, (3) radiological exposure controls.

- Serve as Emergency Control Officer for the designated personnel processing area under F.E.M.A. plan.

- Maintain understanding of exposure, radioactive material transport, radioactive liquid transfer.

- Maintain skills in radiological and environmental testing.

AWARD: Received commendation from superior and cash bonus performance award.

ADDITIONAL: Employment while in college: Sales, Math Tutor, Child Counselor.
Available for travel or relocation as needed.
References provided on request.

Michael Dodd

1825 Union Street, #4
San Francisco, California 94123
Residence/Message: (415) 555-2643
24-Hour Message: (800) 555-7011, ext. 27

EXPERTISE:

Sales / Marketing / Promotions / New Business Development

Proven performer with demonstrated ability to gain account loyalty and win preferential treatment for products. Personable and enthusiastic, able to organize and focus the efforts of others. Strengths include:

- Educating account management and floor sales staff on product.
- Creating special events and public relations activities.
- Designing promotional and incentive programs.
- Following through on organizational details.
- Maintaining a positive, fun image.

EXPERIENCE:

<u>Napa Valley Wines & Spirits Co.</u>, Napa, California, 1987-Present
Account Executive, San Francisco

Selected to manage 50 high-profile accounts in downtown San Francisco. Built close, personal relationships with key management in each account, creating a genuine bond of friendship and mutual purpose.

Accomplishments:

- Designed, coordinated, and managed on-site wine tastings and luncheons. Created innovative promotions such as casino night, winery tours, and other account relations activities. Supported accounts by attending, organizing, or sponsoring special events, fundraisers, house parties, and similar.
- Obtained account participation in maximum number of supplier or wholesaler programs. Facilitated participation by serving as liaison between all parties. Followed through on every account to ensure service on the sale.
- Used former career in F&B to gain buyers' trust due to understanding of their businesses. *Created increased sales for accounts,* which leads to loyalty and greater participation in upcoming promotions and programs.
- Increased wine sales by 75% over prior year.
- Increased liquor sales by 14% over prior year.

Sample Accounts:

- Splendido's
- Postrio
- Bistro Roti
- Bix
- Corona Bar & Grill
- Masa's
- Bentley's Oyster Bar
- Big 4
- Kuleto's
- Grand Hyatt & other major hotels

PRIOR: **Bar Manager,** 565 Clay Restaurant, San Francisco
Bartender, Modesto Lazone's, Opera Plaza, San Francisco
Bartender, Scomas Restaurant, San Francisco

TRAINING & EDUCATION:

Beringer Wine Seminar (3-day professional seminar in the winery)
Beringer Train-the-Trainer Seminar
Robert Mondavi Tasting Seminars
B.S., Geology, James Madison University, Harrisonburg, Virginia

---

REFERENCES ON REQUEST

Ruth Ann Waters

1351 Seminole Street, #6
Miami, Florida 33133
(305) 555-5946

OBJECTIVE: **Word Processing / Secretarial / Clerical / General Office**
- Efficient, good natured, good reputation with all former employers.
- IBM PC, 10-key, transcription, proofreading. (Type 60 wpm.)
- WordPerfect, MultiMate, WordStar. IBM & Mac environments.
- Fast learner.
- Accurate.

EDUCATION: Miami/Dade Community College, Miami, Florida
Associate of Arts (Major: **Word Processing**)   expected 9/91

Hialeah High School, Miami, Florida
Diploma (Honor Student)   6/85

EXPERIENCE: United States District Court, Miami, Florida
(while student)   **Secretary**   1990-Present

- File memos, find and copy cases from law books, type correspondence, maintain office supplies, enter cases on computer. Successfully perform all duties in an atmosphere where accuracy and the ability to follow detailed orders is critical. Cleared three-month backlog in three weeks.

Host Systems, Miami, Florida
Office Assistant   1989

- Entered data on Macintosh computer. Ensured accuracy and completeness of data to be entered. Maintained clean and well-organized office. Also served as the office courier.

Lechter's Housewares, Miami, Florida
2nd Assistant Manager   1989

- Managed store in absence of Manager and Assistant Manager. Opened and closed registers. Balanced daily receipts. Ordered some merchandise. Sold and supervised. Earned rapid promotion.

Cruise Time, Miami, Florida
Office Assistant   1988-1989

- Maintained account information on IBM PC: accounting, billing, and client information. Typed invoices. Answered incoming phones. Handled all errands as courier.

Alcott & Andrews, Miami, Florida
Stockperson   1987

Ross Department Stores, Miami, Florida
Floor Sales Associate   1985-1986

REFERENCES ON REQUEST

Leander M. Hamilton II

23 Pinehurst Circle
Denver, Colorado 80235

Telephone/Message:
(303) 555-2286

PROFILE:

F & B Operations (multiunit or major operations, including resort and hospitality)

Background of proven success in entrepreneurial restaurant/F&B endeavors. Combination of M.B.A. financial skills, staffing and operations expertise, and marketing/promotions savvy. Experience features timely involvement with trendy, formula restaurants, as well as grounding in highly controlled, corporate fast-food operations. Strengths include:

- Concept, image, and menu development.
- Design of policies and procedures.
- Training of management-level staff.
- Training of operations-level staff.
- Quality assurance (top-to-bottom, end-to-end).
- New product development.
- Operational control (waste control, food and labor cost control, inventory and cash control).

Other strengths include extensive experience with international kitchen and work crews, and knowledge of international foods. "Kitchen proficiency" in both French and Spanish.

EDUCATION:

Golden Gate University, San Francisco, California
M.B.A., International Management

Culinary Institute of America, Hyde Park, New York
Certificate, Professional Chef Training & Kitchen Management

California State University, Sonoma, California
B.A., English and **B.S., Political Science** (double degree)

MANAGEMENT EXPERIENCE:

The Palm, Barbados, West Indies   1989 - 1990
Consultant

Start-up consultant on this new restaurant. Contributed to all stages: concept and image development, restaurant design, construction supervision, equipment layout and installation, menu development.

- Hired and trained original staff. Trained chef and asst. chef on recipes.
- Succeeded with extensive negotiations and lobbying with local government officials to win necessary regulatory approvals.
- Completed business launch under projected budgets.
- Achieved positive cash flow for the owner and turned over the operation as scheduled. Excellent recommendation available.

continued . . .

Leander M. Hamilton II *Profile / Page 2*

Taco Bell Corporation (Pepsico), Sacramento, California 1986 - 1989
General Manager

Assigned the highest volume restaurant in the Sacramento region.

- Achieved 24.5% cost of sales, bottom-line operating profit in excess of 32.25%.
- First unit in region to break $1 million in sales.
- Raised Quality Assurance scores from the F to C range to a quad B.
- Facilitated R&D for new product roll out.
- Appointed to the Manager Review Board.

Leander M. Hamilton Associates, San Francisco, California 1983 - 1984
Restaurant Consultant

- Clark's, London, England. Start-up consultant. Set up kitchen and menu. Trained initial chef and kitchen staff.
- Polo Lounge, Bangkok, Thailand. Marketing consultant. Developed marketing plan to attract more tourist and American clientele. Revised bar list.
- The Carlysle Club, Barbados, West Indies. Redesigned bar operations at popular nightclub.

Mill Restaurant, Barbados, West Indies 1982 - 1983
Manager

Hired to turn around negative sales trend in established restaurant with good name recognition but uneven operations.

- Increased profit margin from negative to 28%
- Reestablished relations with better hotel and tour operators.

Le Parite Restaurant, Coconut Grove, Florida 1981 - 1982
Manager

- Achieved a 3-Star rating, one of the very few in the state.

COOKING EXPERIENCE:

Guest Chef, Narsai's, Kensington, California

Sous Chef, Commercial Club, San Francisco, California

Line Cook, Scandia Restaurant, Los Angeles, California

ADDITIONAL:

Additional experience in Europe, West Indies, Southeast Asia, Caribbean.

REFERENCES ON REQUEST

RUSSELL JACKSON

6750 La Cienega Boulevard
Los Angeles, California 90056

Telephone/Message: (213) 555-9044
Telephone/Message: (415) 555-0199

OBJECTVE: **Chef** for a first-rate house.

STRENGTHS:
- Demonstrated command of food basics, technique, philosophy:
  Nouvelle, Classical French, Mediterranean
  Spa Cuisine, California Cuisine
  Regional Mexican Cuisines
  Creole and American Soul
  Chinese and Italian
- Well organized, clean, fast, extensive background of exhibition cooking. Team player: able to take direction, able to give direction.
- Management skills include costing, ordering, hiring and supervising staff, waste control, inventory control, etc.

PROFESSIONAL TRAINING:
Professional Chef Training
California Culinary Academy, San Francisco, California
- Expected Graduation: Spring 1991
- Currently have Honors Standing
- Student Body Representative (three terms)
- Selected to Participate in Restructuring of Curriculum

EXPERIENCE:
Citrus on Melrose, Los Angeles, Spring 1990
Externship
- Apprentice Chef for externship.

Private Clients, Los Angeles and San Francisco, 1986-Present
Contract Chef and **Catering Supervisor**
- Have cooked for Bernie Casey, Sean Penn and Madonna, the Sheen brothers, Kurt Russell and Goldie Hawn, Barishnikov, Kim Bassinger, the Jacksons, Rutger Hauer, Collman Andrews, the Shaffers, U.S. Ambassador to Thailand, and certain well-known San Francisco philanthropists.
- A-list chef and catering supervisor for Opts Catering since 1989. Parties of up to 1200 guests.

Fennel on Ocean Boulevard, Santa Monica, Fall 1988
Line Cook

Rebecca's, Venice Beach, May 1987 - Aug. 1988
Line Cook (still serve as **Guest Chef** when in L.A.)

Border Grill on Melrose, West Hollywood, Dec. 1986 - May 1987
Line Cook

City Restaurant on La Brea, Los Angeles, Nov. 1986 - Jan 1987
Host

Crayons Bar & Grill on Pico, Los Angeles, Nov. 1985 - March 1986
Assistant Manager

PRIOR:
- **General Manager, Vertigo,** Los Angeles
- **Management Trainee, Hard Rock Cafe,** Beverly Center, L.A
- **Line Cook, Stratton's Bar & Grill,** Westwood
- **Executive Chef, Cadillac Cafe** on La Cienga, Hollywood

Chapter 12
Special Styles, More Tricks

Some industries have evolved their own distinctive résumé styles. If your résumé is not in the appropriate style for your industry, then you will look like an outsider *even if you have the right experience*. For instance, believe it or not, airplane pilots and ship captains have their own style of résumé. In this chapter, we will investigate a few of the more common style variations.

Technical

Much has been made of technical résumés, and there are even whole résumé books devoted to the subject. The beauty of the profile style of résumé writing that you have just learned is that it automatically makes for a good technical résumé. Technical résumés feature the candidate's technical skills right at the top. Under that, the work experience is listed just the same as in any other résumé: company, title, scope, accomplishments. You already have a good technical résumé written if you have followed my instructions to this point. Here are two profiles that would be typical for technical résumés:

PROFILE:

Network Controller with wide range of other telecomputing/data telecommunications experience and strong combination of technical and communication skills.

ADVANCED SKILLS:

Hardware:	AT&T Dataphone II
	CODEX
	General DataComm
	3725, 327X, 317X
Software:	NCCF, NPDA, VTAM, NCP, JCL
	MVS/XA, TSO/ISPF, VM/XEDIT, VM/SCRIPT
	NETVIEW, NPM
Specialist:	IBM SNA network installation and maintenance.
	Some experience in network design.

PROFILE:

Hospitality MIS Systems—Installation, Training, Support

◆ Effective combination of technical and communication skills. Experience includes conversion planning, business analysis, installation/implementation, diagnostics and troubleshooting, user training, telephone consulting, and follow-up support.

◆ IBM S/36 & S/34, NCR 2160, Xeta, Northern Telecom SL1, Spectradyne, Teletron Energy Management System, Extel Comexpert Telex, IBM PC, and IBM PS/2.

◆ Hotel Information Systems, IBM SSP & Utilities, NCR FSS, Northern Telecom X.37 & X.11, Xeta, IHC Global Reservations, Delphi Sales & Catering Systems, Acom Bookkeeper/ Inventory, Chouinard and Myhre P/R, ATS, and most common PC applications.

◆ Available for travel and relocation as needed.

Some professions and industries have a distinctive look to their résumés that is hard to describe, but easy to show. Immediately following the narrative of this chapter are full-size samples of résumés that illustrate the points mentioned below. You may want to refer back and forth between the narrative and the samples to really get a feel for the different styles.

Legal   Samples: Andrew Baxter Clay, Barbara J. Damlos

Attorneys' résumés are distinctive, but legal secretaries, paralegals, legal office administrators, and others in the legal field use standard résumés and should follow the résumé instructions elsewhere in the book.

If you are an attorney, you should never put an objective on your résumé; you *are* your objective. Profiles are also rare, but if you have a specialty you can list it with a heading like one of these:

    EXPERTISE: Corporate Taxation
    EMPHASIS: Employment Law
    INTEREST: Environmental Law

Always write "v." instead of "vs." and "judgment" instead of "judgement." Understatement is definitely the preferred tone; brevity is the rule. It's also a good idea to put something interesting somewhere on these résumés, to keep them from looking like ten thousand others. Note the nonlegal job on Andrew Baxter Clay's résumé. Include journal publications and published opinions if available, as shown on the Barbara J. Damlos résumé.

Finance   Samples: Elizabeth Whitney-Wingrove, E. Edleff Schwaab

Finance résumés look a lot like attorneys' résumés, especially on the East Coast. This style may or may not have a profile, and small type and expansive white space contribute to the distinctive look. Most jobs in this sector are gotten by personal introduction and word of mouth, so résumés are noticeably less flashy than in other industries. On the West Coast, finance résumés tend to look more like regular business résumés. Most commercial bankers, insurance executives, and others in fields related to finance should design their résumés with a standard profile and appearance.

Curriculum Vitae (medical, scientific, academic)   Sample: Joshua D.F. Gordon, M.D.

A curriculum vitae, or c.v. as it is commonly known, is a highly stylized type of résumé. Education always comes first, and job descriptions can be extremely brief or nonexistent. Full listings of publications are a common feature, and this style can run on for pages if poorly arranged by the candidate. Although there are many variations, Dr. Gordon's c.v. is a classic example. Note the human interest listing at the bottom, to distinguish this résumé from hundreds of others.

Advertising   Sample: Mary McHale

Advertising résumés always list clients and account teams on which the candidate has served, and little else. Ironically, the résumés of copywriting geniuses are just plain lists of accounts and campaigns. At the entry level, you will want to apply your eloquence to a skills-based résumé as fully described in prior chapters, but once you have any experience at all, simply listing your accounts is the standard style. Public relations résumés are similar to advertising résumés. Prominent listings of accounts are standard, but so is featuring your skills and abilities more fully. Compare Mary McHale's résumé in this chapter with the public relations résumé from Paul E. Davis in the previous chapter.

Acting and Modeling
Sample: Andrea Tipton

Acting résumés are simply tables of performances. They are designed to fit onto the back of an 8 × 10 photograph, usually a head shot. The younger and less experienced the actor, the more training, church plays, and nebulous listings will be featured. As their careers progress, actors list only their best and most recent work, but always on an 8 × 10 sheet of paper. Acting résumés never list an actor's address. It will show the phone number only, or the phone number and address of the actor's agency. Modeling résumés are almost identical, just listing shoots, products featured, and usually the name of the ad agency thrown in for good measure. Height and weight are standard listings, but race is never listed.

Art, Music, TV, and Film
Sample: Bruce Golin

Studio musicians, TV and film people, cartoonists, and those with similar talents often have careers that consist of an unending series of projects, or "credits." Bruce Golin's is an example of a credits-based résumé, which is a good solution for this type of background.

Artist's Bio
Sample: Martha Paulos

An artist's bio is a short biographical statement about her life and philosophy of art. This type of bio is particularly useful as it can be displayed in a gallery along with the artist's work. When applying to galleries, a bio like this would be paired with a credits-style résumé showing training and a list of prior shows and awards. No address or phone is on the bio when it is hung at a show, as all contacts should be made through the gallery.

Consultant's or Speaker's Vita
Sample: Nathaniel A. Robertson

Similar to an artist's biography, consultants' and speakers' vitae are third-person promotional pieces. (Vitae is the plural of vita.) These vitae are designed to be used in marketing a firm, justifying a firm's high fees, and introducing the principals at speaking engagements. Most speakers' bureaus write vitae like this on every speaker they represent. Note that this style is most clearly *not* to be used for getting a job.

"Shuffle the Deck of Cards" Résumé
Sample: Barbara Hermann

Ms. Hermann's résumé is the trickiest one in this book. Note how the repeated use of the subheading "duties" allowed all the work histories to be written in the present tense. With the dates omitted, every single one of these jobs is interchangeable. They can be rearranged and resorted endlessly! We dropped and resorted jobs completely out of order to create this presentation and several others. I would not recommend this for most candidates, but this client reported that she got *tons* of interviews and multiple offers with this résumé. Simply amazing.

Recent College Grad–No Work History
Sample: Danaelle Watkins Bell

This candidate has never worked for pay for one day in her life, yet following the guidelines in this book, she has put together a compelling first résumé. (On technical grounds, this résumé does not belong in this chapter because it does not show any new tricks or styles. However, if I did not point out the candidate's complete lack of paid work experience, you probably would not notice anything unusual about this résumé at all.)

Functional Résumé
Sample: Jeanine Kjömpedahl

A functional résumé, also known as a topical résumé, has the candidate's duties and accomplishments *from all jobs* lumped together under categorical headings such as "Accounting" or "Human Resources," then lists all the employers and job titles at the bottom, with or without dates. The sample featured in this book is a modified functional résumé, because I have distilled my client's skills and built a traditional profile for her on top of the functional categories. For support positions, this style will still get interviews and jobs. As a matter of fact, this résumé gets this client a new job about twice a year.

Housecat   Sample: Ernie

This résumé was written by my associate, Susan Hall. It proves that with a little imagination you can write a good résumé for *any* background and *any* objective.

Andrew Baxter Clay

10 Downing Street, Apt. 2T　　　　　　　　　　Office: (212) 555-6800
New York, New York 10014　　　　　　　　　　Residence: (212) 555-8395

Member of the Bar, State of New York, admitted 1988

EDUCATION

legal　　　HARVARD LAW SCHOOL, Cambridge, Massachusetts
Juris Doctorate, June 1988
　　Activities: Editorial Staff, *Journal on Legislation*
　　　　　　　　Law School Council: Committee to Renovate the Student Union
　　　　　　　　Ames Moot Court Competition

college　　NORTHWESTERN UNIVERSITY, Evanston, Illinois
Bachelor of Arts, History, 1985
　　Honors:　Phi Beta Kappa
　　　　　　　Hearst Award (highest department GPA)
　　　　　　　Graduated with honors for senior thesis analyzing the relation-
　　　　　　　ship between poplar culture and public policy in the context of
　　　　　　　the "Star Wars" program.

preparatory　CAIRO HIGH SCHOOL, Cairo, Illinois
　　Honors:　Valedictorian
　　　　　　　State Debate Champion

EXPERIENCE

legal　　　ASCHER, ELIASSON & RHEIKHART, New York, New York
Attorney, August 1988–Present
　　Member of trial team for the $2.1 billion Texoil pollution coverage litiga-
　　tion. Managed numerous smaller matters. Prepared and argued motions.
　　Defended depositions. Currently carrying the major responsibility for a
　　multimillion-dollar commercial dispute between a corporate insured and
　　its insurer.

ASCHER, ELIASSON & RHEIKHART, New York, New York
Summer Associate, July-August 1987
　　Prepared summary judgment motion. Researched and drafted memo-
　　randa for corporate and litigation matters. Observed depositions.
　　Received permanent offer.

ISHAM, LINCOLN & BEALE, Chicago, Illinois
Summer Associate, June-July 1987
　　Researched and drafted memoranda for numerous cases. Received perma-
　　nent offer.

HIGGS, FLETCHER & MACK, San Diego, California
Law Clerk, Summer 1986
　　Researched and drafted memoranda for personal injury and business liti-
　　gation. Drafted settlement conference brief, orders, and trial briefs for an
　　attorney malpractice case.

non-legal　BAUMAN FARMS, Reese, Michigan
Farmer, Summers 1983, 1984, 1985
　　Operated 200-acre farm on profit-sharing basis. Drove and maintained all
　　equipment. Made crop marketing decisions. Earned full tuition for junior
　　and senior years of college, and first year of law school.

BARBARA J. DAMLOS

1800 Greenwich Street
San Francisco, California 94132

Office: (415) 555-6451
Residence: (415) 555-1636

EXPERIENCE

MISCIAGNA & COLOMBATTO, San Francisco, California   1/85-Present
Partner

Insurance defense litigation in the areas of insurance coverage, insurance bad faith, personal injury, and products liability. Drafted appellate writs.

Published opinions:
Bodenhamer v. Superior Ct. (G.A.B.)(1986)178.Cal.App.3d.180
Bodenhamer v. Superior Ct. (St. Paul)(1987)192.Cal.App.3d.1472

Primary responsibility for trial preparation. Assisted lead counsel in four-month trial of insurance bad faith case.

TOLPEGIN, IMAI & TADLOCK, San Francisco, California   Fall 1984
Law Clerk

Directed discovery in toxic tort litigation. Researched and drafted pleadings, motions for summary judgment, and discovery requests.

BIANCO, BRANDI & JONES, San Francisco, California   5/83-5/84
Law Clerk

Researched issues in unfair competition, trade secrets, product liability, and insurance bad faith. Reviewed personal injury and malpractice cases.

HANCOCK, ROTHERT & BUNSHOFT, San Francisco, California
Law Clerk   Summer 1982

Researched legal issues in bankruptcy proceedings, construction actions, and insurance coverage cases involving asbestos-related claims.

HANCOCK, ROTHERT & BUNSHOFT, San Francisco, California   7/80-8/81
Paralegal

Assisted in preparation of two major construction cases for trial.

EDUCATION

UNIVERSITY OF SAN FRANCISCO SCHOOL OF LAW
Juris Doctor   1984
Law Review
Semi-Finalist, Advocate of the Year Competition, Moot Court
    Honors Program
First Place Award, Oral Advocacy, Moot Court Competition

UNIVERSITY OF CALIFORNIA, DAVIS
Bachelor of Arts, Political Science (minor: U.S. History)   1980
Dean's List, Prytanean Honor Society
Intern, State Department of Consumer Affairs, Sacramento
Intern, Public Citizen, Ralph Nader Organization, Washington, D.C.

PUBLICATION

The Duty of Good Faith—More Than Just a Duty to Defend and Settle Claims,
14 Western State University L.Rev.209 (Fall 1986)

AFFILIATIONS

Member of the Bar, State of California
California Trial Lawyers Association
Bar Association of San Francisco

(please keep this application confidential at this time)

Elizabeth Whitney-Wingrove

600 Quincy Street, #110
Boston, Massachusetts 02125

24-hour Telephone/Message:
(617) 555-8311

EXPERIENCE

financial   **M.P. Handel & Co., Inc.,** 3/83-Present
Boston, Massachusetts
Institutional Equity Sales Trader, 9/85-Present

Service 30 major institutional investor accounts. Solicit trades, execute trades, develop client relationships, distribute research product, sell investment ideas. Recent concentration has been educating clients on our foreign products, including settlement operations and capital commitment services. Completed intensive research project on international program trading.

Selected to take over the entire account base of a senior partner, a total of 76 accounts. Completed two months advanced training in New York. Currently travel approximately 30% to key accounts and company offices in New York, Philadelphia, Washington, and London.

Sales Assistant to Research Salesperson, 3/83-9/85

Assisted in sales and client services related to analysts' reports on 15 selected industries. Included direct client interaction at all levels, planning/hosting/coordinating meetings and social engagements for institutional investors. Provided administrative and technical support. Coordinated with New York and Washington offices. Retained through several mergers: M.P. Handel, Smythe & Holden, Rowe & Pitman.

prior   **Lanier Business Products, Inc.,** 1980-1981
Chicago, Illinois
Senior Sales Representative, Corporate Accounts
Top Producer.

Weather Tamer, Inc., 1978-1979
Chicago, Illinois
Assistant Marketing Director

Huntington Industries, Inc., 1978
Chicago, Illinois
Cost Analyst

Bullocks Wilshire, 1976-1978
Los Angeles, California
Senior Assistant Buyer

EDUCATION   **M.B.A.,** Finance, Boston University, 1983
B.S., Fashion Retailing, Purdue University, 1976

CREDENTIALS   **N.A.S.D. Series 7** (Series 63 pending)

REFERENCES   References and additional information provided on request. Please keep this application confidential at this time.

E. Edleff Schwaab

1250-F Piccadilly Place, White Plains, New York 10601
(914) 555-5820 (home), (800) 555-2406 (work)

EDUCATION: NEW YORK UNIVERSITY, New York, New York
M.B.A., Finance, *summa cum laude* 1983

SYRACUSE UNIVERSITY, Syracuse, New York
B.S., Accounting, *magna cum laude* 1980

CREDENTIAL: **CFA Candidate**
Level I (passed) 1989
Level II (results pending) 1990
Level III (anticipated) 1991

EXPERIENCE: MAHAN, ROMANSKI & O'CONNOR, INC., New York, New York
Portfolio Manager / Securities Analyst 1990-Present

Comanage a publicly traded, diversified high income mutual fund. Developed the original investment strategy, prepared marketing material, and selected investments for the fund. Performance has led to an eightfold increase in assets under management in the fund to $8 million in the first 7 months. This fund is currently performing third out of 86 high-yield funds as ranked by Lipper.

Also prepare general investment analysis for this firm, which has $1 billion total assets under management. Conduct fundamental research, communicate with management and sell-side analysts, and assess economic and industry trends. Select and monitor investments in the following sectors: banks, S&Ls, insurance, airlines, aerospace, machinery and equipment, diversified companies, convertible bonds, and high-yield bonds.

EMPIRE FINANCE SAVINGS BANK, Riverhead, New York
Senior Investment Analyst 1988-1989

Comanaged $100 million high-yield bond portfolio. Recommended investment decisions. Prepared written and oral presentations to CFO, CEO and Chairman on strategies and ideas. Sole liaison to management of companies under investment, sell-side analysts, and traders.

TPFM&C (a Towers Perrin Co.), New York, New York
Senior Financial Analyst 1984-1988

Developed models, projected cash flows, and valued a range of potential mergers, acquisitions, divestitures, LBOs, and alternate capital structures. Developed and analyzed long-range financial and business plans.

Developed methodologies and financial models to analyze 9 acquisitions and 9 divestitures worth over $1.5 billion, which were approved and consummated according to plan.

ASHLAND OIL, Pittsburgh, Pennsylvania
Senior Financial Budget Analyst 1980-1984

Developed, analyzed, and interpreted corporate operating and capital budgets. Supervised 3 Financial Analysts.

ACTIVITIES: Competent Toastmaster (CTM), Toastmasters International
New York Marathon (last eight years)

JOSHUA D. F. GORDON, M.D.

Curriculum Vitae

820 Mill View Lane
Los Altos Hills, California 94022

Telephone:
(415) 555-0132

SPECIALTY: Anesthesiology

CREDENTIALS:

Board Eligible, American Board of Anesthesiology	1990
Basic Life Support Instructor	1990
Advanced Cardiac Life Support	1990
Diplomate, National Board of Medical Examiners	1987
Federal Licensure Examination	1986
Medical License, State of California	1985
Medical License, State of Ohio	1984

EXPERIENCE:

Staff Anesthesiologist (part-time)

Santa Clara Valley Medical Center, San Jose, California	1990-1991
Pacific Presbyterian Medical Center, San Francisco, California	1990-1991
Sonoma Valley Hospital, Sonoma, California	1991
Seton Medical Center, Daly City, California	1991

TRAINING:

Research Fellowship (blood bank and liver transplant anesthesia)   1990
University of California, San Francisco

Residency (anesthesiology)   1987-1990
University of California, San Francisco

Internship (internal medicine)   1986-1987
University of California, San Francisco

EDUCATION:

M.D., College of Medicine   1986
University of Cincinnati, Cincinnati, Ohio

A.B., Biochemical Sciences   1982
Princeton University, Princeton, New Jersey
   Thesis: *Studies on a Deletion Mutant from a Recombinant Bacteriophage Library*

Three Advanced Levels (physics, chemistry, biology)   1978
Twelve Ordinary Levels   1976
Harrow School, Harrow-on-the-Hill, England

continued . . .

RESEARCH:

ARTICLES:

The Pharmacokinetics of Vecuronium During Liver Transplantation in Humans. J.D.F. Gordon, M.D., J.E. Caldwell, F.F.A.R.C.S., M.C. Prager, M.D., M.L. Sharma, Ph.D., L.D. Gruenke, Ph.D., R.D. Miller, M.D., *Anesth Analg* 1990; 70: S432 (abstract, presented at the IARS 64th Congress, Honolulu, Hawaii, March 13, 1990).

Vecuronium Plasma Concentrations During Orthotopic Liver Transplantation in Humans. J.D.F. Gordon, M.D., J.E. Caldwell, M.B.Ch.B., M.C. Prager, M.D., M.L. Sharma, Ph.D., L.D. Gruenke, Ph.D., D.M. Fisher, M.D., N. Ascher, M.D., Ph.D., R.D. Miller, M.D. (submitted).

The Effect of Aprotinin on Intracranial Pressure and Cerebral Edema in Rabbits with Galactosamine-induced Acute Liver Failure. J.D.F. Gordon, M.D., M.C. Prager, M.D., S.F. Ciricillo, M.D., M. Grady, B.A. (submitted).

A Comparison of HTLV-1 Seropositivity in Orthotopic Liver Transplant Recipients Before and After Routine HTLV-1 Screening. J.D.F. Gordon, M.D., E. Donegan, M.D. (in preparation).

ADDITIONAL:

Fibrinolysis During Liver Transplantation, in association with Dr. Marie Prager, Department of Anesthesia, Dr. Marc Schuman and Dr. Larry Corash, Department of Hematology, UCSF, 1990.

Analysis of Lymphocyte Subset Variations Associated with Liver Transplantation, in association with Dr. Elizabeth Donegan, Director of Blood Bank, UCSF, 1990.

AFFILIATIONS:

American Society of Anesthesiologists	1988-Current
International Anesthesia Research Society	1988-Current
California Society of Anesthesiologists	1988-Current
Northern California Anesthesia Society	1988-Current

COMMUNITY SERVICE:

Volunteer, Animal-Assisted Therapy Program, San Francisco SPCA	1989-Current
Instructor, Basic Life Support, American Red Cross, Southwest Ohio Chapter	1985-1986

PERSONAL INTERESTS:

Interested in therapeutic aspects of animal-human relationships, especially as related to illness recovery and geriatrics. Hobbies include Weimaraner dogs and violin. Certified Grade VIII (Final) "with distinction" in violin, Board of Royal College of Music, London.

Mary McHale

615 Marina Way
Sausalito, California 94040

Office: (415) 555-2000
Residence: (415) 555-7166

EXPERIENCE:

FOOTE CONE AND BELDING, San Francisco, California, 1968-Present
Senior Broadcast Buyer / Spot Account Manager

Place over $15 million per year in broadcast time for such clients as:

- Mastercard
- California Raisins
- Levi Strauss
- Mazda
- Pacific Bell/Pacific Telesis
- Supercuts
- Mattel
- Ashton-Tate
- Alaska Tourism

- Albertsons
- C&H Sugar
- Colgate-Palmolive
- Adolph Coors
- Universal Studios
- Citicorp
- Clorox
- ARCO
- Eddie Bauer

- Long John Silvers
- Dreyers Ice Cream
- California Milk Advisory Board
- Hughes Airwest
- Orion Pictures
- Payless Shoe Source
- Farmers Insurance
- First Interstate

Buy for up to 47 markets simultaneously. Have bought over 200 rated markets in the U.S. and Canada, with emphasis on:

- San Francisco
- New York
- Atlanta
- Cleveland
- Cincinnati

- Seattle
- Dallas
- Phoenix
- Philadelphia
- Honolulu

- Sacramento
- Kansas City
- Tampa
- Las Vegas
- Minneapolis

Skills include:

- Analyzing, negotiating, purchasing, maintaining, and monitoring radio and TV buys. Additional skills include post analysis, client contact, and training of assistant buyers.

- Negotiating radio and TV sports sponsorship packages for clients, including TV and radio schedules, promotions, and merchandising programs.

- Serving as liaison with buyers, planners, account management, and clients, including contact with FCB regional offices.

Prior experience provides well-rounded background:

- Assistant Media Buyer (one year), Commercial Production Account Coordinator (two years), Print Production Coordinator (two years).

EDUCATION:

Holy Names College, Oakland, California

REFERENCES:

References and recommendations citing skill and professionalism provided on request.

ANDREA TIPTON

(SAG, AFTRA)

Frederick & Templeton Agency, Inc.
6608 Hollywood Boulevard, Hollywood, CA 90028
(213) 555-8506 {in New York, call (212) 555-6100}

DATA

Height: 5'7"	Hair: Blond	Ages: 23-35
Weight: 115	Eyes: Blue	Lang: Italian, Polish, Greek

FILM

When Harry Met Sally	Waitress	Rob Reiner, Dir./Castle Rock
Zelda	Zelda	Paul Scott Reuter, Dir./ NYU Student Film
Bye Bye Budapest	Mrs. Borbas	Margeaux Wasommer, Dir./ WSU Student Film

THEATRE

The Snow Queen	Snow Queen	Long Beach Players/Long Beach, CA Deborah La Vine, Dir.

"A visual delight—a female Mr. Spock," Heffley, L.A. Times
"A beautiful, regal Snow Queen," Warfield, Drama-Logue

The Woolgatherer	Rose	New Studio Theatre/Detroit, MI
A Midsummer Night's Dream	Titania	Mullady Theatre/Chicago, IL
Uncommon Women	Rita	Mullady Theatre/Chicago, IL
Lysistrata	Corinthian	Mullady Theatre/Chicago, IL
Rattlesnake in a Cooler	Ellen	Detroit Repertory/Detroit, MI
Who Killed Richard Cory	Mistress	Fourth St. Playhouse/Royal Oak, MI
Quail Southwest	Kerra	Fourth St. Playhouse/Royal Oak, MI
The Late George Apley	Lydia	Henry Ford Theatre/Dearborn, MI

COMMERCIALS

List upon request.

STAND-UP COMEDY

At My Place	1990	Santa Monica, CA
Igby's Comedy Cabaret	1990	Los Angeles, CA

TRAINING

The Groundlings	Improv	Los Angeles, CA
Judy Carter	Stand Up Comedy	Los Angeles, CA
Greg Dean	Stand Up Comedy	Los Angeles, CA
Lawrence Parke	Scene Study	Los Angeles, CA
Loyola University	B.A., Drama, 1986	Chicago, IL, and Rome, Italy
Lodz Film School	Acting	Lodz, Poland
Kosciusko Foundation	Acting	Warsaw, Krakow, Wroclaw, Poland

Bruce Golin

4366 Monroe Avenue, #107
Studio City, California 91604

Telephone:
(818) 555-0575

PRODUCER/CO-PRODUCER

STRENGTHS:

- Twelve years in television—great record for on-time and on-budget.
- Good communicator with writers, talent, crew, production and post-production techs.
- Strong on directing/shooting inserts and 2nd Unit filming.

CREDITS:

Adam-12/Dragnet (New Syndicated Series), The Arthur Company, 1990-Present
  Position: Producer
  Executive Producer: Burton Armus

The Smothers Brothers Comedy Hour–20 Year Reunion (CBS), Comedic Productions, 1988
  Position: Associate Producer
  Executive Producers: Tom and Dick Smothers—Producer: Ken Kragen

Pee Wee's Playhouse (CBS Series), BRB Productions/Pee Wee Pictures, 1987
  Position: Production Manager
  Executive Producer: Steve Binder—Production Executive: Howard Malley

We Are the World (USA for Africa), Golin-Malley Productions, 1985
  Position: Stage Manager
  Exec. Producers: Ken Kragen, Ken Yates—Producers: Craig Golin, Howard Malley

Knight Rider (NBC Series), Universal Television, 1984-1986
  Position: Associate Producer
  Supervising Producers: Burton Armus, Bruce Landsbury

Simon & Simon (CBS Series), Universal Television, 1982-1984
  Position: Assistant Associate Producer
  Executive Producer: Phil DeGuere—Producer: Richard Chapman

Legends of the West (ABC Special), Marble Arch Productions, 1981
  Position: Production Coordinator
  Producer: Eric Lieber

The Gambler (CBS Movie of the Week), Kenny Rogers Productions, 1979
  Position: Production Coordinator
  Producer: Ken Kragen

The Lily Tomlin Show (NBC Special), Tomlin Productions, 1979
  Position: Production Coordinator
  Producer: Rocco Urbisci

EDUCATION:

Pre-Med, University of California, Los Angeles

Martha Paulos

Montreal
Canada

---

*"I like snakes; they're flexible and
come in all colors." — Botero*

Martha Paulos is a Montreal artist known for her sculptures of animals and plants, all of which she calls paintings. Her brightly colored representations exhibit a pervasive sense of humor and a strong sense of the unusual in the mundane. The emotive impact of her works is initially humorous, hiding a more concealed cynicism that adds a depth unknown to many young artists.

A full decade of formal study behind her, Ms. Paulos claims to be most influenced by American and Mexican naive and primitive art. Secondary influences include Flemish portraiture and Italian Renaissance painting.

Ms. Paulos produces unavoidably interesting sculptures of cacti, people, dogs, snakes, and other animals, and has recently begun to produce a series of houses. Having focused on nearly lifesize pieces, she is now moving toward developing arrangements of her independent characters into total environments.

With five years of serious exhibitions, Ms. Paulos is an emerging and prolific artist, and has already won a significant award for one of her dog sculptures, a yellow pit bull with a snake in his mouth. She has pockets of aficionados throughout Canada and the U.S., shows regularly in New York, and is just now beginning to attract the attention of serious collectors.

As a thoroughly modern artist, Ms. Paulos is refreshingly accessible. Now at the Lumina Gallery, Quebec City, P.Q. (418) 555-1942.

Robertson & Associates

Attorneys-at-Law
3801 Melrose Avenue, Suite 1500
Los Angeles, California 90029
(213) 555-4964 or (213) 555-1713

Nathaniel A. Robertson
BIOGRAPHY

Nathaniel A. Robertson is a graduate of Stanford University and the University of California at Berkeley (Boalt Hall) School of Law. He is a member of the ABA, the NBA, and the CBA, and is licensed to practice before all California State Courts, Federal District Court, and the U.S. Court of Appeals. Mr. Robertson is well known in legal and business circles in both Northern and Southern California. He has been described by at least one media source as a "major force in West Coast litigation."

Mr. Robertson is currently the principal of Robertson & Associates, a law firm specializing in quality legal research and representation concerning matters of banking, securities, commercial credit and tax law, general business and contract litigation, professional liability, personal injury, product liability, appellate services, and such related services as negotiations, advocacy memoranda, and representation to tax, government, or regulatory authorities.

In addition to heading his law practice, Mr. Robertson serves as a private consultant to banks and fiduciary entities. He provides advisory services, structuring, and oversight for a wide range of transactions and agreements, for both corporations and financial institutions. This includes projects for such institutions as the European Industrial Development Bank and more routine assistance to such entities as the Arbuckle Consulting Group, the renowned Southern California venture capital firm.

Prior to starting his firm, Mr. Robertson was Founder and Executive Director of the Western Legal Research Institute at Stanford for seven years. WLRI is a legal think tank and support firm providing quality research, writing, and analysis to private practitioners, corporate counsel, and attorneys in government. Mr. Robertson built a team of dynamic young attorneys around this new concept, and this "law firm's law firm" gained quick recognition as both innovative and highly resourceful. WLRI has continued to grow and has been touted as the model of a new breed of legal services firm.

WLRI provides litigation, research, and analysis in the areas of administrative law, automobile injury, banking, civil procedure, civil rights, commercial law and bankruptcy, constitutional law, contracts, corporate law and antitrust, criminal law and procedure, eminent domain, energy, environmental law, family law, labor law, pension benefits, copyright and trademark, personal injury, product liability, real property, securities, torts, trusts, wills and estates, and workers' compensation.

Mr. Robertson's earlier career spans assignments as research attorney for the California Supreme Court and research clerk/fellow/extern for Public Advocates, Inc., Honorable Justice Frank M. Newman, Pacific Gas and Electric Corporation, National Aeronautics and Space Administration, Legal Aid Society of Alameda County, and the U.S. House of Representatives Subcommittee on Equal Rights.

Barbara Hermann

2310 Rio Grande Street
Houston, Texas 77040

Telephone:
(713) 555-3125

PROFILE:

Administrative Assistant

- Career secretary, administrator, and front and back office staff person. Over 15 years in office environments. Extensive PC computer experience.

- Skilled in all general office: typing, filing, word processing, data entry, light bookkeeping, clerical, invoicing, writing/editing documents and correspondence.

- Also skilled as front office and/or executive assistant: screening calls and visitors, routing mail and deliveries, maintaining calendars, and managing travel arrangements.

HISTORY:

Gulf Coast Salvage & Recycling, Houston, Texas
Office Administrator
Duties:

- Handle all administrative, secretarial, and clerical support for plant. Manage large cash fund and accounting records. Prepare weekly/monthly production reports. Data entry.

The Sharper Image, Houston, Texas
Authorizations Representative, Credit Department
Duties:

- Verify credit card data for phone and mail orders. Communicate with customers and banks.

Monadnock Building Associates, Dallas, Texas
Administrative Assistant
Duties:

- Receptionist for the management office of this high-rise building. Handle lease administration, accounts receivable ledger, correspondence, and secretarial duties.

Latch Management Services, Dallas, Texas
Receptionist
Duties:

- Front desk receptionist for this management consulting firm. Requires advanced interpersonal and client relations skills, in addition to general office.

Blue Cross of Texas, Galveston, Texas
Clerk/Typist/Customer Service
Duties:

- Clerk/Typist, Third Party Liability Clerk, Customer Service Representative for Hospital and Professional Liaison Unit and Correspondence Unit.

EDUCATION:

Certificate, Secretarial Studies, Mrs. Caldwell's Business College, Tulsa, Oklahoma

DANAELLE WATKINS BELL

3736 Lakeland Avenue
Minneapolis, Minnesota 55422

Telephone / Message:
(312) 555-4972

INTERESTS: **Editing, Writing, Research.**

STRENGTHS:
- Technical command of the English language: grammar, syntax, semantics, spelling, punctuation.
- Experience in copyediting and proofreading according to *The Chicago Manual of Style.*
- Significant experience in primary research; very resourceful at finding data and developing primary and secondary sources.
- Wide-ranging knowledge of history, politics, cultures, and science.

EDUCATION:
degrees

University of Colorado, Boulder
B.A., History December 1990
- Graduated magna cum laude.
- Thesis: *Cinderella Learned to Fly: An Examination of Women Aviators of WWII.*

Shady Side Academy, Pittsburgh, Pennsylvania
Diploma May 1986

activities

National Outdoor Leadership School
Leadership Training Spring 1988
- Baja California survival and ecology trip.

University of Pittsburgh, Pennsylvania
Semester at Sea Fall 1987
- Traveled around the world on the U.S.S. Universe.

symposia

Magazine Writers' Symposium Fall 1990
Aspen Writers Conference Summer 1990

EXPERIENCE:

University of Colorado, Boulder 1989–1990
Researcher (senior research project)
- Collected data from across the country on women aviators of World War II. Researched primary and secondary materials in USAF National Archives and other government sources.
- Found and interviewed women veterans. Visited USAF Academy to record views of women cadets of today.
- Wrote 80-page academic thesis.

University of Colorado, Boulder Fall 1989
Instructor's Assistant
- Selected by the Head of the Astrophysics Department to serve as student aide.

University Hill Elementary School, Boulder, Colorado Fall 1988
Tutor
- Reading and writing tutor.

TRAVEL:
- Bicycled in New Zealand; traveled in Australia, Thailand Spring 1991
- Traveled in Europe Spring 1989
- Bicycled through Great Britain Summer 1988
- Kayaked in Baja California Summer 1987

Jeanine Kjömpedahl

129 Windview Terrace Place, #108   Telephone / Message:
Albuquerque, New Mexico 87123   (505) 555-0174

CAREER DIRECTION: Seeking **Secretary/Administrative Assistant/Office Manager** position utilizing a strong combination of analytical, interpersonal, and leadership skills.

TECHNICAL SKILLS:

IBM PC	**Typing** (65 wpm)	**Lotus 1-2-3**
WordPerfect	**Transcription**	(hands-on)
SuperCalc	**Editing**	**MultiMate**
WordStar	**Proofreading**	(hands-on)
Wang OIS-50	**Bookkeeping**	

EDUCATION:

Certificate, Word Processing   1990
Southwest Community College, Albuquerque, New Mexico
- Advanced training on WordPerfect release 5.1.

Certificate, Office Technology, certified *with honors*   1988
Control Data Institute, Albuquerque, New Mexico
- Maintained 95% GPA. Award for "Outstanding Attendance."

Economics and **Business Administration**   1981-1985
University of New Mexico, Albuquerque
- Completed 3½ years toward B.S. in Economics while working full time.

EXPERIENCE:

Administration & Office Management
- Prepared and modified large cost proposals, including multiple-variable contract modifications using Lotus 1-2-3 for engineering contracts.
- Worked as only office, administrative, and bookkeeping person on major construction site, including control of large petty cash fund on site.
- Posted accounts receivable, maintained general ledger through trial balance. Researched and reconciled all accounts.
- Supervised computer and clerical staff in Look Back and TAA medical research, tracing former patients using national databases such as TRW.
- Consistently demonstrated telephone and organizational skills.

Interpersonal & Leadership
- Contacted former patients and informed them of potential exposure to AIDS virus. Demonstrated caring and compassionate manner.
- Achieved high volume of sales in straight-commission sales positions.
- Coordinator and Chair for "Employee Day."
- Made collection calls for a major jeweler.
- Received *numerous* letters of commendation from associates about my work.

Technical
- Strong technical/analytical aptitude. Experience as laboratory technician, hospital equipment technician, and in other medical-oriented assignments requiring mathematical/statistical skills.

HISTORY:

Secretary/Office Manager, Mark Diversified Contracting, Inc.	current
Administrative Assistant (PR), Veterans Memorial Hospital	1989
Administrative Clerk, Carpet Connection	1988-1989
Equipment Technician, Veterans Memorial Hospital	1987-1988
Sales Associate, Standard Shoe Store	1985-1986
Administrative Specialist, Thames Temporary Agency	1983-1984

ERNIE

Alley #3
Corner Market & Broadway
Megopolis, New York 10012

OBJECTIVE:

Long-term position as **Housecat.**

QUALIFICATIONS:

- Omnivorous. Strong rodent-control capabilities.
- Excellent nonverbal communication skills. Highly developed purring mechanism.
- Affectionate. Adaptable. Rare feline willingness to follow established guidelines.
- Proven stud potential.

EXPERIENCE:

BARNCAT, Westchester Estate, New York   March 1988 - May 1990

Ensured day-to-day rodent and small animal control for two-story, 35,000 sq. ft. barn.

- Consumed average of over 5 rodents per day.
- Achieved 37% reduction in barn swallow population.
- Awarded feline leukemia inoculation after 1 month of service.
- **Earned in-house privileges for outstanding service and deportment after only 2 months on the job!**

ALLEYCAT, Wilshire Boulevard, Los Angeles, California   November 1986 - February 1988

Successfully maintained territorial boundaries of 4 sq. block area in notoriously competitive and dangerous location. Developed high degree of proficiency in urban survival, hunting, and scavenging skills.

- Honored by co-cats for consistent expertise in maneuvering safely and adroitly through heavy skateboard, auto, and roller-skate traffic.
- Known sire of at least 77 feline litters over 9-month period.

EDUCATION:

Certificate, Feline Deportment   January 1987
TOM & JERRY ASSOCIATES, Hollywood, California
   (1-year intensive with Tom of famed "Tom & Jerry" partnership)
   High Honors

REFERENCES:

Enthusiastic recommendations provided on request.

Chapter 13
HOW TO GET INTERVIEWS; HOW TO PLAN AND MANAGE A JOB SEARCH

A job search is like a game of chess: It has an opening, a middle, and an end game. You use different strategies in each stage, and you watch every moment for an unexpected opportunity to seize and exploit.

First, you build a strong opening position, creating a network from which to launch multiple attacks on your objective. In the middle, you must keep track of a large volume of possibilities, and an error can turn the tide of the game against you. In the end game, you must sustain your advantage, close in on your target, and win.

This chapter explains how to launch and manage a successful full-scale, no-holds-barred job search. If your needs are different, just scale back your activity, but do not fail to heed the counsel on job search protocol, momentum, and timing.

First you must make a personal decision to plan and manage your job search aggressively. Decide to commit resources to your job search, especially *time* and *money*. Make sure you have the raw ingredients: an answering machine; a typewriter or access to a fast and responsive secretarial or word processing service; plenty of résumés, stationery, second sheets, envelopes, stamps, paper, 5×8 cards, and an inexpensive postal scale; an appointment book, and a decent place to work.

Even if you decide to use your kitchen table as the "command center" for your job search, you must have access to it; it should be clean and well organized, and the project should not have to compete for your attention with jelly drippings or proximate TVs.

Also, as you begin to get interviews, you will need to have a perfect personal appearance. That means at least one complete outfit, from topcoat to umbrella. Now *is* the time to splurge and buy a new suit of clothes. Pay attention to details and accessories. Do your watch and your shoes fit with your job objective? Do your clothes fit you as you are today? If money is a real problem, borrow the items you need to complete the outfit. You can buy your own "career accessories" after your new job improves your cash flow.

Clothes are far more important than you might want to believe. They really do need to be *perfect*. It is no accident that the word "suit" is a synonym on Wall Street for a junior executive. ("Get me three suits by Monday. I need to start that new cold-calling campaign!") It is even a good idea to scout the company before your interview to see how people at your level dress, and imitate them.

Do not muddle through this project with halfway measures. The result is your future. Look good, and you will feel good and be confident.

Building a Lead List

Your first task is to build a lead list. There are four main sources for job leads:
- Networking
- Cold contacts
- Headhunters and agencies
- Newspapers

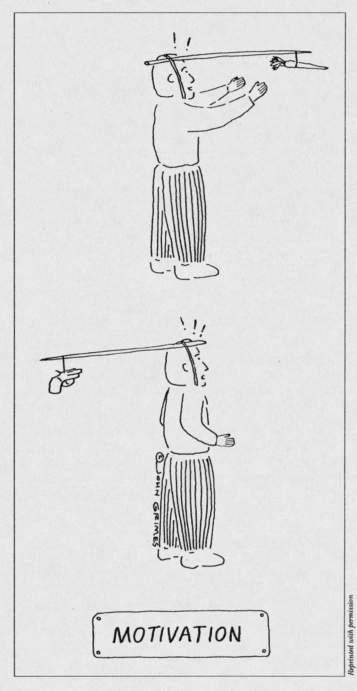

MOTIVATION

Reprinted with permission

Build as big a lead list as you can. Be open-minded. This is your opening game, and you do not want to concede resources before you even assess their potential value. I think of these four sources of job leads as the four wheels on an automobile. I would not recommend that you drive a car very far on three wheels, and I would not recommend that you conduct a full-scale job search without developing and exploiting job leads from all four of these sources.

Networking is easy. Your targets are everybody you could call on the phone by name. That includes *at least:* everyone in your family, all your neighbors, all your friends current and past, all the members of every club or organization to which you belong, every employer or fellow employee of every company at which you have ever worked, all the suppliers and clients with whom you have worked, and every college peer or professor you ever had, and *all their friends and acquaintances.*

This is a pretty big list. For most of us, this is several hundred people.

At all levels, from migrant farm workers to the top echelons of the business elite, some version of personal referral is the number one source of the job lead that results in employment. I will tell you what to do with this list in a moment.

———◆———

Next, make a list of companies that you would like to contact. Do not make a fanciful wish list of companies you know nothing about. A good way to start is to make a list of your current employer's vendors, clients, and competitors. Do not forget that the majority of new jobs (entry- to executive-level) are created in smaller businesses, not Fortune 500 companies.

Another good source is the business press. If you do not read the trade press for your industry, call them tomorrow morning and subscribe. The articles not only provide you with companies, but with truly important information like line managers' names, titles, and current pet projects. In any case, you want to be able to talk intelligently about your industry, and reading the trade press is a must.

If your list of companies is still short, you can always walk into the business branch of your local library and ask the reference librarian for help. There are association directories, industry directories, compilations of local employers by size and industry, all types of data available. Every listing will be a trifle dated, however, and you should verify everything from the corporate headquarters address to whether they have gone Chapter 7 since the last update. (See section 2, "How to do Research on Companies" in the bibliography.)

If you live in a major metropolitan area, there are several publishers producing regional how-to-get-a-job books complete with company listings, names of key personnel, and similar data. Walk into any major bookstore and ask for a book like this for your region. Remember, every piece of data you read will need to be verified before you can use it.

Needless to say, this list of companies will overlap your list of networking contacts. That is, some of your contacts will work at these companies. That is fine. You will launch multiple attacks on these targeted companies anyway.

———————

Headhunters, employment agencies, college placement offices, and your state employment development department are more sources of job leads. The preceding list is roughly in order of the level of job they represent. The higher up the business ladder you are, the higher up the list you should look. Everyone should contact his or her college placement office once in awhile, but state agencies can be full of out-of-date listings for nightmare jobs.

There are many books written on headhunters alone. If you know the headhunters who specialize in your industry, you definitely should use them. If you are currently employed *and* you are making more than $60,000 per year *and* your career has shown rapid advancement in the last five years, then you definitely should contact them. Otherwise, they may not be a good source for you. They still could be, but the odds get considerably slimmer.

Headhunters broker a *lot* of jobs between $35,000 and $60,000, but they work more like agencies to do it. The old maxim was "Agencies find jobs for people; headhunters find people for jobs." In practice, though, the line between employment agencies and executive recruiters has all but disappeared in most states. If your salary falls between $35,000 and $60,000, you could find yourself working with both. Do not expect a lot of frills and handholding in this range.

I would definitely recommend that you avoid any organization that wants you to pay a fee, but otherwise, depending on your level, you should make some targeted contacts in agencies or recruiting firms. Warning: If you want to switch careers, placement specialists are not going to be too excited about speaking with you.

You can look in the yellow pages under Executive Search Consultants for headhunters, under Employment Agencies for agencies. A better trick is to call the directors of human resources for major companies in your industry and ask them what headhunters they use. Of course, while you are asking, you may as well ask for an informational interview at the same time.

If you are a solid executive-level candidate, call Kennedy Publications at (603) 585-6544 and ask for *The Directory of Executive Recruiters*. This book is rarely available in bookstores. Mention Résumé Righters℠ when you call; they will take your credit card over the phone and send your directory out the same day. This directory is a little complex, but you will be able to sort executive recruiters by industry, function, and location. The Recruiting & Search Report publishing company will do a computer sort for you for a very reasonable fee; call (800) 634-4548 or (904) 235-3733.

I will tell you what to do with the list later, but try to target agencies and recruiters that work with people like yourself.

———————

If you are management level, check the newspaper only once a week, on Sunday for most metropolitan papers, although Monday is also a big career day in some markets. Tuesday is the conventional day for listing new management positions in the Wall Street Journal. You may wish to subscribe to the *WSJ*'s *National Business Employment Weekly*, a compilation of the job ads in all four regional editions of the *WSJ* combined with topical articles on job searching at the management level. Call (212) 808-6792 or (800) JOB-HUNT to subscribe.

If you are a lower-level candidate, check the papers every day. Caution: No one should use the papers as his sole source of job leads. Be sure to use the other sources discussed above as well.

The newspaper is a good place to get ideas and to get a feel for the job market in your field. Also check industry and trade publications, which usually have some kind of career want ads section. Advertisements have a bad reputation as a source of job leads, the result of two unrelated facts: first, many of the most important career books in the last decade were written by headhunters, and, second, advertisements generate considerable competition for you, the candidate.

Headhunters have a vested interest in coming between you and the in-house recruiters at companies. Obviously, this prejudice does not concern you.

If you have followed the straightforward instructions in this book, your résumé will win against heavy competition. If you are a good candidate with a good résumé, you have nothing to fear.

———————

Build as large a lead list as you can. Your lead list, your résumé, and your telephone are the most important keys to your next job.

The Telephone Is Your Best Friend

To paraphrase former Chicago Mayor Daley, "Call early and call often." Call all your networking contacts and alert them to your job search. Tell them what you are looking for, and ask them if they have any ideas. Ask them to keep an ear out for any leads, and be sure to tell them you will be calling them back next week. Then do it. It is also a good idea to send them a copy of your résumé with a short note, reminding them of your call. Give them permission to forward the résumé to interested parties. (Remember, this plan is for a full-scale job search. If you are employed, you may wish to think twice before spreading your résumé from coast to coast.)

Do not ask your contacts for a job; ask for ideas and referrals. This is called lowering the ante. Likewise, when you begin to contact employers, ask for ideas, introductions to third parties, information, informal interviews, brief meetings, conversations, anything but a job. Asking for a job puts them on the spot. When you lower the ante, your contact is genuinely relieved, and that relief translates into a greater willingness to help you with a meeting or a viable job lead.

If a targeted employer says they are not hiring, you have two options. Ask to interview anyway. Say something like, "Even if you don't need anyone now, I'd like you to know what I have to offer. Then if something opens up, you'll think of me first." Or, you can ask for an informational interview about the position that is not open, and the company and industry in general. Use this type of contact to gain intelligence about the type of position you are interested in and to get referrals to other companies or divisions or departments where you might be needed now. The fact that a company is not hiring has no bearing on its potential value to your job search.

———◆———

Whether you have a lead on an opening or a lead that could lead to a lead on an opening, you approach all contacts roughly the same way: Call and get the exact name, title, and mailing address of your key contact. Try to get a little information on the opening, if there is one. Do this in every case except when responding to a newspaper ad that demands "no calls." If you can find a network lead into a company with a "no calls" ad, by all means, call, cite your network connection, and proceed as though you had never seen their ad. Do not hesitate to approach a company at multiple levels and through multiple channels, especially large companies. I have had clients receive routine rejection slips from companies long after they started to work there.

Send in your résumé and cover letter addressed to your contact, then call back. The simplest thing to ask is if she got it. If not, great, you have an excuse to call again. Say who you are, tell her you will send another one, then call back again.

Use these calls as an opportunity to inquire about their hiring process. I am an advocate of total honesty. If someone asks you who you are and what you want, tell them in as honest and forthright a manner as possible. You will be surprised at their willingness to help you. Ask what are the most important criteria for the position, find out who is making the decision and how their interview cycle works, ask everything you need to know to be a good candidate. Be sensitive to their needs. Always ask, "Is this a good time to ask a quick question, or would you rather I call back?" Right when a company first opens in the morning is the best time to call. Call before the company even opens and you can often reach the owner or a top officer working early.

If I were launching a job search myself, I would not bother to send a letter or a résumé to anyone without calling first and without calling to follow up. Then, unless you decide you do not want the job, *ask for an interview.* Do not wait for them to decide to interview you, ask for an interview! Remember to lower the ante. Say something like, "That sounds very interesting. Do you think I could stop by to talk about it, at your convenience of course?"

If this sounds simple, it is. This is it. This is how you get interviews. You call and ask for them.

The telephone is your best friend. Use it.

Job Search Protocol, Momentum, and Timing

One of the most important aspects of a job search is momentum. I once worked with a very talented CFO who blew lead after lead by failing to follow up in a timely manner. He thought a week was fast enough to get out a follow-up letter. He thought three or four days was fast enough to return a call. Time after time, I saw the hiring authority's excitement fade before my candidate made his next move.

Timeliness is next to godliness. You must call within thirty-six hours after your material lands on the desk of your target. After thirty-six hours, your application, letter, or idea is dead meat. Nobody can find it, nobody knows anything about it, and nobody cares. So be prompt, create urgency, demonstrate how "on top of it" you are.

Obviously, to gauge thirty-six hours from "on the desk" time, you need some way to tell when your mailing will arrive. The U.S. mails have become the dumping ground for second- and third-class junk. Even first-class mail between two buildings in the financial district can be totally unreliable, with delivery varying between one to four days. And you have to allow some time for the company's internal mail distribution system, another variable.

Consider alternate delivery. Within a city you can send your résumé by messenger. These ubiquitous carrier pigeons can penetrate well into companies, placing your envelope right on the desk of the person you seek. Write directly on your 9×12 envelope, "URGENT—via MESSENGER." Then call the next morning. If you are applying to another city, use an overnight courier service. Then call the morning after it arrives.

Try to avoid faxing your résumé. It will not look very sharp on fax paper, and the alternate delivery routes mentioned above are almost as fast and far more attention getting. Do not fax your résumé to companies you have not contacted personally. Nothing could be more annoying than an unwanted fax from somebody who cares so little about the company that he could not pick up the phone and call first.

———————◆———————

Although the following points are probably overwhelmingly obvious to you, I have been surprised that many people do not know them:

Never, never, never send a résumé without a cover letter, or a fax without a cover sheet. The best thing that can happen is it will get lost before it can damage your reputation.

"If I should come to work for you, Mr. Hysop, I could transform this organization overnight."

Never use stationery, envelopes, or the postage meter from your current employer. It smacks of disloyalty, and is, in fact, theft. However, feel free to use your business cards.

Never put any comment about salary requirements in a cover letter. You will disqualify yourself automatically from jobs you might enjoy. Many employers can be convinced to pay far more than they planned if they like you, but they are not going to like you very much if you do not give them a chance. This is a quintessential example of a throw out factor. Ironically, you may even disqualify yourself from a higher salary for the job you eventually accept. If you do feel compelled to comment on salary, speak in vague ranges, not exact figures. Still, it is better to reveal this information later. Remember, you are not supposed to be sending your résumé out to anyone you do not plan to call.

Always show up for meetings five minutes early. If you are held up at one interview, call the next one and reschedule it for the next available time rather than going in late. If you are unemployed, be careful that your internal clock does not get "loose." I worked with a displaced vice president of a major bank. Early in the search he showed up five minutes early for everything, but as the project wore on, he began to act as though 9:08 were the same thing as 8:55. **It is not.**

Never say anything bad about a former employer. If you are very angry at a former employer, only practice will allow you to say nice things about him. Practice with your spouse, your dog, your rearview mirror. Say only nice things, out loud. You really do have to do these rehearsals; otherwise, you will blow opening night.

Avoid any attitude that can be interpreted as "I don't know how you can get by without me." This is evident in such common statements as, "I know I will be an invaluable asset to your organization," or "I know I could solve that $54 million marketing problem for you within six months." Employers find this attitude presumptuous and offensive. Of course you want these things to be true, but to say them outright is a mistake.

Instead, find out how you actually would fit into the organization and discuss how your skills would be applied. If there is a fit, both you and your potential employer will know it.

If you are not at the management level, and your job skills are readily available in a large number of other candidates, then timeliness can be everything. In some markets you can buy the Sunday paper on Friday or Saturday. Get your letters in the mail by Saturday night, and they will start arriving Monday morning. Your potential employer will be impressed, and may even wonder how you could respond to an ad in the Sunday paper on the Saturday before.

Better yet, hand deliver your résumé the moment the company opens on Monday. Do not be pushy in asking for an impromptu interview, as many business people view unnecessary interruptions about the same way a horse views a snake.

If youth, vitality, and eagerness are your main job qualifications, you cannot apply too early, follow up too exactly, or be too polite. Do not succumb to the temptation to concoct a "creative" résumé; every employer has a drawer full of these things, all from people she has never interviewed.

Make a straightforward, skills-based résumé. If you want to be creative, use an unorthodox delivery system. Everybody knows the story about the scriptwriter who threw his opus over the producer's pool fence. I would not bother people at home, but have you considered rolling your résumé up, tying it with a silver ribbon, tossing it in a mailing tube so it has a nice rattle, and sending it via messenger marked URGENT?

Of course, none of these tricks will work unless you pick up the phone and follow up with a call.

As an alternate point about timing, at the management level I do not recommend jumping on newspaper ads. You may seem desperate. You might want to wait until the ad is about a week old, or more. As a general guide, you can reply to newspaper ads up to four weeks late. Sometimes you can even miss the first or second cut by doing this. Here is one of my favorite lines, which can be used to give the impression that you have not been looking for a position at all: "One of my friends alerted me to your recent advertisement ..." With this line, you can respond to ads weeks late. Be prepared to name the friend in the interview.

The hiring cycle at some companies is longer than you could imagine. Even if they have placed someone in the position, sometimes that person does not work out, and your application arrives just as that becomes apparent. Or the person they hired may hire *you*, as she rebuilds the management team. Be open to these possibilities, and view newspaper ads as just another way to get into a company. Once you are inside, you can look in all directions for the right fit.

Always call one day in advance to confirm your appointments. It is also a good idea to discuss the objectives of the meeting. I had a client who was a whizbang at translating computer science and mathematical research papers from German, Dutch, and French into English. He won an interview with Apple Computer at a time when Apple had cult status in Silicon Valley. Everybody wanted to work there, and Apple was practically begging my client to come down and interview.

He had an appointment with *five* key executives. Five department heads were going to converge and meet with this candidate. Five management staff members were planning to disrupt their schedules for him. His human resources person, the one who had coordinated this affair, the one whose you-know-what was on the line, called him to confirm the meeting. Something was wrong with his tape machine, so he never got the message. And he never called. He showed up five minutes early alright, but it was too late. The atmosphere was hostile, the meeting did not go smoothly, and they decided they had better find themselves another whizbang.

———————•———————

After every interview, do two things:

First, write down what happened, with attention to the interviewer's key concerns. For example, the last person to hold the job may have been dynamite at organization and follow-through, but lousy at dealing with irate clients on the phone. So the hiring authority's key motivator may be your customer-service skills. You will need detailed notes to remember these keys as you continue to have a large volume of interviews and contacts.

Then, *that very same day*, write a short, sincere thank-you note and get it into the mail. Your interviewer will be most favorably impressed to receive this promptly. (Messenger or courier service may seem pretentious for this follow-up, so use the mail and hope.) For lower-level positions, a tasteful card may be sufficient; at middle to higher levels, a typed note on monarch-sized stationery is acceptable. If the interview and the company are both informal, you may decide that a *readable* handwritten note will be sufficient. Under no circumstances should you write by hand on a full-sized sheet of paper. You must type a more formal thank-you letter if you use this size of paper.

Another use of a follow-up letter is to address some issue brought up in the interview, or to recoup from some *faux pas*. If the interviewer thought you lacked direct outside sales experience, this might be a good time to drive home that you were the largest-selling cookie monster the Girl Scouts ever had in the state of Iowa. I think you get the picture.

Needless to say, in any interview you should ask about their hiring process, how many interviews they plan, what the competition is like, and when they plan to make their decision. At the end of the interview, ask, "When will I see you again?" or "When should I call you back?" Never leave the ball entirely in their court.

Be nice to everybody. Turn every dead end into a new networking lead. Tell them you will check in with them in a week, just in case. Then do it.

It is rare to get a management job in less than three interviews, and up to seven interviews is not uncommon. Job search protocol has become more important than ever, with executive positions going to the Emily Post crowd over better qualified, but less polished, applicants. You must care about these details and attend to them promptly, or the position will go to someone who does.

Organizing and Managing the Search Project

Now that you have some understanding of what you will be doing in your job search, you can see that this is a lot of detail to manage. You will have to track and control this large project, with hundreds of potential contacts. You will soon find that John is out of town, Jane cannot come to the phone right now, Peter is not the one you should talk to after all, and so on.

I recommend that you use a simple mechanical tool: 5×7 cards. I have had clients build databases on their PCs which they can sort by multiple fields and keys, but 5×7 cards will work just fine. Alphabetize by company or contact name, whichever you remember best, and then sort by *date of next activity*. You can make your notes directly on the card. John will be back on May 23. At 8:55 A.M. on May 23, you will call. Jane's secretary said call back

PIONEER PLATE GLASS
2703 Industrial Way   555-2613
contact: Tom Angstadt, Production Engineer, Springfield Plant
- called 8/7/90, spoke re positions as cost analyst, referred me to Chris Smythe ♂ in account
- called C. Smythe, 8/7/90, out of town til Monday
- called C. Smythe, 8/13/90. "not available" left message
- called C. Smythe, 8/14/90. — "in a meeting"! left message
- 8/14/90, 4:30 PM. called Tom Angstadt back, asked him to call C. Smythe
- 8/15/90, called C. Smythe @ 9 AM. "not available"
- called T.A. back, asked him again, he said he'd do it right then
- 9:30 C Smythe called, we spoke of cost analyst position, he said he didn't need one, but send resume anyway. Resume mailed 8/15/90, PM
- called C. Smythe 9 AM 8/17/90. got resume. nice conversation. he was interested in my experience in payroll. Appt set for next Weds.
- 8/22/90. met C. Smythe. Good meeting. Met CFO Lawrence Steadsitter. goes by "Larry". toured Springfield plant. Met plant mgr. Charles Johnson — "Chuck" seems to be really informal place
- Said he had projects for cost analyst — not full position. sent follow up letter to Steadsitter, ① offering to do the projects on contract, & ② asking to apply for other accounting openings. sent note to C. Smythe
- 8/27/90. called Steadsitter. good talk set mtg for 3 PM with plant manager and Smythe. wants to create bridge position, ½ cost analyst, ½ staff accountant
- JOB OFFER!! 8/27/90 6 PM

tomorrow. Tomorrow you will be sure to call. And so on. On this page is a sample notation card. Remember, you might have *hundreds* of these cards active at once.

Set quantified goals for new applications each week; follow-ups do not count. A goal of as few as ten applications per week will soon snowball into a rolling mass of details and follow-up tasks. You must set an ambitious goal for new applications, or you will soon find yourself busy as heck with nothing really going on. You will think things are going great, but your job search could start to wind down before you get any offers. Set *specific, quantified* goals in advance for new contacts per week, then track and check your performance.

Balance your time between your four sources of contacts: networking, direct contacts, headhunters and agencies, and the newspapers. Put up to 50 percent of your effort into networking and personal referral, but no more than 25 percent into any other one source.

Take every Friday afternoon off from your job search, but set aside Sunday evening to review the last week and to plan the next one. If you have not met your quota for the week, you can respond to some of the ads in the Sunday paper to meet your quantified target for new applications. If possible, have a friend call or stop by on Sunday night, every Sunday night, to whom you will make a report of your activity. Even better, find two or three people who are also looking for employment and start your own job club.

I once worked with a gentleman leaving the Air Force who formed such a job club with three of his friends. I wrote his résumé and his three friends copied the style perfectly. They each read one get-a-job book and reported on it to the others. Their searches were as professionally thought out and well managed as any I have ever witnessed. Their group served as a crucible for ideas and a place to share the ups and downs of the job search process.

Once You Start to Get Offers

No matter what, do not stop sending out new applications! Meet your quota for new applications right up until the day you start your new job.

SUNDAY NIGHT SCORECARD - THE JOB SEARCH WEEKLY REPORT

LIST OF <u>NEW</u> CONTACTS: (ten minimum)
1)

2)

3)

4)

5)

6)

7)

8)

9)

10)

n)

NEW CONTACTS FROM NETWORKING:
(up to 50% of total effort)   _____   _____
                                                     number   % of total

NEW CONTACTS FROM COLD-CALLING:
(up to 50% of total effort)   _____   _____
                                                     number   % of total

NEW CONTACTS WITH HEADHUNTERS & AGENCIES:
(no more than 25% of total effort)   _____   _____
                                                     number   % of total

NEW CONTACTS FROM ADVERTISEMENTS:
(no more than 25% of total effort)   _____   _____
                                                     number   % of total

---

LIST OF FOLLOW-UP ACTIVITY: (should be more than one page, *at leas*t)

FIRST INTERVIEWS:

CALL-BACK INTERVIEWS:

OFFERS:

GOALS FOR NEXT WEEK:

If you get an offer, make sure it is a firm offer. Ask point blank, "Are you offering me the position?" If so, ask, "On what terms?" If you have a firm offer for the job you want, accept it and get something in writing before you leave. Obviously, this is easier if you have calculated in advance what you consider to be your minimum salary and other terms you would require.

If you have a firm offer and are not positive you want it, it is perfectly within bounds to say you need to sleep on it and you will call them tomorrow. Be sure the offer stands! On more than one occasion I have seen a candidate come back to accept an offer that either had never been formally extended or had been withdrawn because it was not accepted immediately. If you stall more than a few days, most employers will retract the offer, with or without telling you.

If the position is not right for you, decline it. You learned a lot in applying for it, and you can use that experience in your continuing search for a position that *is* right for you.

Salary Negotiations

The general rule about salary is to bring it up as late in the game as possible. Do not respond to a written request for salary history before you have an interview. Acknowledge the request by noting "Salary: Negotiable" at the bottom of your cover letter, but do not address the issue further. Providing salary data before an interview *can only count against you.*

In the early stages of your interview process, respond to an inquiry about salary requirements or salary history with an inquiry of your own: "What range did you have in mind?" No matter what their response, try to deflect the conversation away from salary and back onto the position or your qualifications. Say something like, "We're in the same ballpark, but I am really more interested in the job and what it entails. Could we come back to this later?"

A similar line is "Well, that doesn't seem unreasonable, but I really need to know more about the position before I could say exactly what I think would be fair."

Another line is "That seems a little low for what you are expecting from this position, but let's talk further because I really like the company and the people I've met so far."

Always speak in vague ranges, like "mid to high fifties" or "something close to six figures." Do not disqualify yourself unless you and the potential employer really are in completely different ballparks. Wait until they offer you a position.

Only when you get a "Yes" to your question, "Are you offering me the position?" should you begin to discuss the issue in earnest. Then, quote your total compensation package.

HOW TO TURN $43,000 INTO $68,800	
Your base pay:	$43,000
Plus your estimated bonus:	$4,000
Plus your next raise, if imminent:	$4,300
Plus the value of your perks:	
Company auto that you drive 25,000 miles per year:	$13,000
Matching contribution to company-sponsored retirement plan:	$2,000
Life and health insurance:	$1,900
Average four sick days each year your company lets you cash out:	$600
Your compensation package:	**$68,800**

Include your company car, insurance, and other benefits in your quote, but focus their quote on cash. *Know the score.* Do not walk into this meeting wondering how much you make now, or how much you will require to accept this position.

Do not lose a job because of salary negotiations. If they will not match your cash needs, get the difference in perks: signing bonus, incentive bonus, club fees, extra vacation, generous retirement fund contributions, child care, fancy insurance, moving expenses, a fat expense account, paid education, you name it. Creativity and flexibility here can keep your career moving along. Rigidity can make the employer think you are afraid to take a risk and can result in losing an opportunity that could have benefited you in the long run.

If a position really contributes to your five-year goals, it is usually a good idea to take it at any salary.

When you finally do accept a position, you are off the market. *No matter what,* you must reject all other offers that come in. Show the same integrity you expect of your employer.

Reprinted by permission of Chronicle Features, San Francisco, California.

Do Not Oversell Yourself

My clients are generally fairly aggressive. They are committed to advancing their careers, and to performing in the positions they take. I have had clients negotiate pay increases as high as $90,000 just to switch jobs. That's right, a *raise* of $90,000. Salary increases of $20,000 to $30,000 are a matter of routine. However, every one of these clients is fully qualified to perform in these new positions.

My goal in this book, and my goal in life, is to get you the best job for which you are qualified, and nothing more. If you apply for jobs for which you have no qualifications, and for which you have not substantiated any material interest, and for which you have not prepared yourself, then you will not succeed.

If you use the tricks in this book ruthlessly, you will find yourself in interviews for positions far beyond your capacity to perform. But do not underestimate your interviewers. They usually can weed you out *in seconds*. If you are really interested in a career path, research it. Find people who are excelling in this field now and ask them how they got into it.

Do not abuse the techniques provided in this book. Use them to get the very best job in which you can excel. Nothing more, nothing less.

Chapter 14.
Cover Letters: Don't Write One
Until You Read Chapter 13

Cover letters serve as routing slips for the résumé. Their primary purpose is to get your résumé in front of a viable contact, and to motivate that contact to read further. The more you concentrate on this function, the "routing slip" function, the more successful your cover letters will be.

Cover letters are usually only read once or twice, to route your résumé to the person who acts on it, and to spur that action. That action may be to throw it away, to file it, to set it aside with a stack of others, to set it aside to wait for your call, or to call you right away. Obviously, you want one of the latter possibilities.

Do not put critical information in only your cover letter. All critical and substantive points belong in your résumé. That is yet another reason the profile style of résumé is so powerful—your skills and abilities are on the document that counts, not on the routing slip!

To control the routing of your résumé you always want to write to a person, not a title, a department, or a company. As explained in the last chapter, you must make your phone calls and get the exact name, title, and address of your contact. If your telephone inquiry is not successful, only then should you resort to writing to a title or department, or *several titles* and *several departments*.

The one exception to the call-first rule is a blind box ad in a newspaper. If you are employed, you should be especially wary of these ads anyway. If you are unemployed or everyone in your company knows you are seeking new employment, then you really have nothing to lose but the postage. If the blind box is a post office box and you live in a major city, your librarian can lead you to a reverse directory and you can crack this screen. Do not hesitate to tell them how you discovered who they were, as you ask to whom exactly you should address your application.

Your response rate will drop drastically anytime you do not address your letter to a particular person. Every company has a standard procedure for processing unsolicited résumés, and it is usually designed to get rid of them. Having your résumé filed for "future consideration" with the human resources department is about as useful as having it sucked into a black hole.

The number-one way to avoid this procedure is to identify your mailing as a "personal" or a "solicited" mailing. In your very first paragraph, cite your telephone call or your personal referral source. Very few clerks are willing to take the risk of sending your material to the black hole if it looks like somebody in the company is expecting it, or you may be somebody important, or know somebody important.

Here are some sample introductory paragraphs demonstrating this technique:

Dear Ms. Jacobs:

I was discussing Hyatt operations with Joseph DiMarco, and he suggested that you might be interested in someone with my background. My expertise is MIS for hospitality businesses. In the interest of discussing employment opportunities with you, I have enclosed my résumé for your review.

Dear Ms. Snyder:

We met a few weeks ago in Chicago at the Ritz Carlton while Nick McRobie was giving you a demonstration of Acom software packages. Ever since our conversation about your aggressive projects to retool for the '90s, I have been thinking about discussing employment opportunities with you. Toward that end, I have enclosed my résumé for your review.

Dear Mr. van den Burgh:

I was discussing my job search with Lars Lundgren recently, and he mentioned you quite favorably. He gave me your current address, and suggested that I contact you directly. Since I saw you last . . .

The same technique works with headhunters. If you are a personal referral, your résumé will be handled differently than an unsolicited mailing.

Dear Ms. Taylor:

I got your name from a professional acquaintance, Mr. Dale Shaw, Director of Human Resources for Majorfees Corp. He said you often have clients who would be interested in someone with my background. Accordingly, I am sending my résumé for your review.

If you are applying to a known opening, cite that opening *as part of your heading*. Try not to make anyone actually read your cover letter in order to tell what position you are seeking.

Attn: Ms. Toni Bonetti, Director, Management Recruiting
Re: Company Representative, Asia/Pacific Markets, advertised in *WSJ,* 11/20/90

If there is a job code in an announcement or advertisement, be sure to feature it in a similar fashion. Companies use these codes to route résumés and track response, so make it easy for them:

Attn: Mr. Clyde Anthony Watkins, Director of Personnel
Re: Staff Accountant, ACC-27-NYT

Cover Letters as an Accessory to Your Telephone

All of the above points will facilitate the routing of your résumé. Now let us consider what else to put in your cover letter. If you know for sure your contact is going to read your résumé, you can keep your letter exceedingly brief, e.g.:

Dear Mr. Witherspoon:

Here is my résumé, as you requested. I will call you by tomorrow afternoon to answer any preliminary questions you may have. In any case, I look forward to meeting with you on Thursday at nine o'clock. Meanwhile, I hope you are feeling better. I had a similar travel experience in Nigeria, but we can talk about that when we meet.

Short letters are usually appropriate for referral contacts, as well:

Dear Charles:

As you requested, I have enclosed a few copies of my résumé for you to forward to potentially interested parties in Hong Kong. I appreciate your assistance, and I'll call you next week to follow up.

Because of the brevity of this type of cover letter, it can look terribly small way out in the middle of a piece of 8½ × 11 paper. It is a good idea to get some monarch-sized paper of the same weight and texture as your résumé for short letters. If that is not possible, just make your own. When you print your résumé, have them cut some of the paper to 7×10, or cut it yourself on a paper cutter. Do not cut across the watermark.

The proper protocol is to staple your résumé together, if it is more than one page, and to paperclip the cover letter to the résumé. I prefer gold-colored paperclips as a nice detail. Even when using monarch-sized paper, I would always type the cover letter. Handwritten letters communicate either intimacy or laziness, and neither is appropriate prior to your first meeting.

Whenever possible, you should use the telephone so forcefully that these short cover letters are sufficient. Not everybody is comfortable being a salesperson for themselves, however. If this is true of you, then your cover letters must do the selling for you.

Cover Letters that Sell

If your letter is going to someone who is not obligated to read your résumé, you will need a traditional cover letter, a sales pitch for you and your résumé. These full-bodied cover letters have three functional parts:

- Introduction
- Rationale, or "pitch"
- Call to action

In your introduction, you say why you are writing. Specify the job or functional area in which you are interested and, of course, drop any names or referral sources right away. Some examples of introductory paragraphs are listed in the sections above.

Remember to lower the ante. Mention that you would like to "discuss possibilities" or "explore the potential for mutual interest." Do not say anything like, "I'll be the best account executive you ever had on your team!"

In the main body of your letter, you *try to set yourself apart from other applicants*. You try to impress your reader with your accomplishments and talents. You can give a logical rationale for your candidacy, or some type of sales pitch for yourself based on the quality of your experience and accomplishments.

If possible, relate your strengths to the requirements of the position, and always gloss over or omit reference to any weaknesses. For example, if the ad specifies "college grads only" and you have no degree, focus on your skills, accomplishments, aggressive sales approach, whatever, but do not mention education at all. The cover letter is no place for excuses or negative points.

Be cautious of boasting that you know a lot about your potential employer's business, and avoid statements like, "I know I would be a valuable asset to your business." If you have not interviewed for the position yet, that is a bit presumptuous, don't you think? We will look at some successful examples in a moment.

In the "call to action" you tell the reader what you want to happen next. Most cover letters, even from very savvy business leaders, lack a definitive call to action. This is the biggest mistake you could make. You must tell the reader what to do next, or suffer the consequences—usually the sorting stack or the black hole.

The number one way to avoid these consequences is to avoid them in advance, by proper use of your telephone. Other techniques all depend on the call to action in your cover letter.

The most effective call to action technique is that of telling your reader you will be calling soon. This always increases your impact on the reader. Nobody wants someone to call and catch them unprepared. Contacts will read your résumé with greater interest, and try to remember your name, *all subconsciously* because they know you are going to call and check up on them.

...ss to say, if you say you will call and you do not, your candidacy is much worse off ...you do not make such a promise in the first place. Do not forget your thirty-six-...me limit. You do not have to say exactly when you will call, but your call is going to ...maximum impact during the first thirty-six hours after your material lands on your ...s desk.

...ker technique, but perhaps more comfortable for you, is to tell them to call you. It sounds simple, but it makes a difference. "Please call me to discuss this further." Without a line like this, without a call to action, your résumé is just one more piece of junk mail, to be sorted and forgotten.

Samples

In all of the following samples, look for the three key functional parts of a cover letter that sells:

- Introduction
- Rationale, or "pitch"
- Call to action

I prefer a cover letter that makes an argument, that in some way gives a rationale for your candidacy. The following letter had a phenomenal response rate for my candidate, even though she did not call and ask for interviews. The reason for her success was the outstanding rationale, which set her apart from the thousands of other, virtually identical candidates.

Dear Hiring Partner:

I am interested in opportunities to serve your firm as a law clerk or extern this summer. I have several things to offer that may be of interest to you:

1. My high grades demonstrate my abilities and my desire to perform on your behalf. I have skills in research, writing, case control. I take my assignments very seriously.

2. Although I am a first-year student, I already have paralegal and legal editing experience. I can be productive without any initial "break-in" period.

3. I speak conversational Japanese. If you do any work with native speakers of Japanese, I could be of benefit. Also, I know Japanese business protocol, which is just as important as the actual language.

I am interested in an opportunity to work closely with talented attorneys. I can offer detailed legal skills in support of their activities, accuracy, and a knowledge of my own limitations.

Please call me at your convenience to discuss this further. It would be a pleasure and an honor to be associated with your firm this summer.

Respectfully yours,

A. Winning Candidate

The following letter is in a style favored by fast-track professionals. It will work with any background with easily quantified bottom-line-type accomplishments. The main body of the letter is a big pitch for the candidate; it *sells* the reader on the candidate's expertise. This particular letter targets a search firm, but could easily be modified to target the head of sales for a company.

Dear Placement Specialist:

I have 18 years of increasing responsibility as a sales rep and sales manager in the food-service industry. If you have any clients seeking someone with this type of background, perhaps you will be interested in these accomplishments:

- Increased volume by 117% for an established company. This was the result of a revitalization of sales efforts. No gimmicks—just hard, smart work.
- Introduced new product to 30,000 pounds in sales in first 90 days, more than 15 times our original target!
- Established sales programs for a new company resulting in 15,000 cases sold in first eight months.
- Earned <u>National</u> Salesman of the Year award in second year with McCormick & Company, a major national company.
- Trained in sales and marketing with Proctor & Gamble.

The above shows a top performer. For additional detail, I have provided the attached résumé for your review. You will see that I have management skills, endurance, and a desire for continued career challenge.

My present company is very happy with my performance, but it has gone through two mergers in the last six months. My position certainly seems to be secure, but I feel it is time for a wise man to consider his options.

If you have anything of interest to discuss, call me at your earliest opportunity. I look forward to speaking with you soon.

Sincerely,

A. Strong Candidate

Whenever you write to a headhunter, demonstrate that you understand how the search business works. Ask for a referral to a client, not a lead on a job. Remember that you are in fact the commodity in this equation. Use lines like this: "Perhaps your timely introduction could be fortuitous for all concerned" or "I should think that any of your clients who are in need of reducing their lead time from R&D to full commercialization would be interested in my accomplishments in this area."

———————

Broadcast cover letters are used for horizontal penetration of a large number of companies. For example, you might use one if you wish to sell your expertise in doing conversions from computer system A to the new, improved computer system B. If you can get a list of all companies who use system A, you can send them a broadcast cover letter with your résumé to alert them to your services.

Of course, calling these same companies and establishing some sort of phone dialogue will be much more effective than just sending out letters.

Here is a broadcast cover letter for a mortgage banking specialist who is in great demand to clean up the seemingly unending chaos surrounding the United States savings and loan fiasco:

Dear (Mr. or Ms. Regional Bank or S&L President or CEO):

As we discussed on the phone, my expertise spans most existing types of mortgage instruments: fixed-rate, ARM, GPM, GEM, and Wrap agreements. I have strong experience with GNMA and FNMA requirements, as well as specialized experience with the FSLIC and RTC.

From the attached you can see that my greatest strength is obviously project management for (1) quality assurance reviews of loan portfolios and various risk management studies, (2) due diligence related to the buying and selling of loans on the secondary market, (3) reconstruction of loan activity, (4) computer and operations conversions and mergers, (5) design and placement of quality assurance measures, and (6) staff training and the creation of a quality-oriented atmosphere.

In addition to project work, I can be available to serve as an interim manager or supervisor as needed.

I will be calling you shortly to discuss your own needs, and to see if you have any questions. Also, I can update you on recent projects as this area of banking continues to be very exciting from an operational point of view.

Thank you for your interest.

Most sincerely,

A. Financial Savior

Broadcast letters can also be used by recent college graduates when they have a fairly well-defined employment target. Again, the letter is used to achieve horizontal penetration of a large volume of employers, and must be preceded by and followed with a telephone call in order to get a positive response.

Dear (Mr. or Ms. Employer):

I am a recent graduate of the University of Illinois bachelors' program in Architecture, including one year of study abroad at L'Ecole d'Architecture et de l'Urbanisme in Versailles.

It is my desire to begin *in any capacity* with a prominent firm. I am eager to work with some talented designers, and you will see that I have a solid base of skills to contribute. I have autocad training, and my drafting, drawing, and rendering skills are sufficient to make immediate contributions to your projects. I am serious about my career, and I am sure you will find my skills and my professional attitude are in line with your high standards.

I am seeking to join a firm that will offer me ongoing challenge and opportunity. My résumé details some of my technical skills, but you cannot tell whether you will be interested in me as a permanent employee until you see my portfolio. I think you will find the work of interest, and it will only take a moment to review the portfolio with you.

In order to see if we have a mutual interest, I will be calling you soon. It would be my pleasure to be available for a brief meeting at your convenience.

Respectfully,

A. Fine Candidate

When applying for a specific opening, you can tailor your entire presentation to the keys in the announcement or advertisement. Do not use a point-by-point response, as this will only highlight your shortcomings. Giving a point-by-point presentation also makes it very easy for the employer to compare your background with others who respond using a similarly structured letter. Instead, read the announcement carefully and see what hints and subtleties you should address. There will be many, many candidates who have the minimum qualifications. You want to be the candidate who answers the employer's unstated but implied concerns.

Develop a prose presentation of your strengths relative to the needs of your target. The bigger the job, the longer your letter can be. The following letter won an interview at odds in excess of a hundred to one, even though my candidate was in Kansas and the targeted reader was a Los Angeles–based personnel consulting firm acting as a screen for the City of Irvine, California.

Dear Mr. Donaldson:

I was interested to come across your advertisement in *JobBANK* for Manager of Cultural Affairs for the City of Irvine, California. I have been seeking an opportunity such as this, and I think you will find that I might fit your job description. I have enclosed my résumé for your review.

My background is in city planning and arts administration, which has proved to be an extremely effective combination. I believe my skills, abilities and accomplishments are represented, albeit briefly, on the enclosed materials.

In checking my background you will find that I have succeeded in two different but equally important areas: providing effective leadership, direction, and management; and making the arts fun and participatory for a very wide range of constituents, from public school students to major benefactors. It is difficult to show "feel good" accomplishments, but you will note that throughout my career I have been able to marshall the support, cooperation, and enthusiasm of an incredibly diverse set of peers and colleagues.

I feel that I have been instrumental in generating long-term benefit for the organizations which I have served, and that benefit can best be summarized as (1) increased financial support, (2) increased public support, and (3) increased organizational efficiency.

I already have good friends in Southern California, and relocation to the area would be welcome. This position is of great interest to me. I think that your client, the City of Irvine, might be interested in my candidacy as well. Perhaps your introduction could be beneficial to all concerned.

Thank you for your attention to these materials, and I'll be calling you very soon to see if you have any questions and to discuss your selection process.

Yours sincerely,

A. Fantastic Candidate

When there is no opening, it is usually a good idea to acknowledge this. Use lines like "I would like to discuss career opportunities with your representative," or, if you want to have an informal or informational interview, "I am not applying for a particular position at this time, I am just interested in discussing possibilities. I'll be calling you soon to see if we can arrange a meeting at your convenience."

Key words to drop into any cover letter are "fit" and "mutual interest." When you manage your career right, you will be interviewing your contact companies just as closely as they will be interviewing you. The more you realize and act on this, the more respect you will get from your interviewers, and the better "fit" and greater "mutual interest" you will find.

You do not have to mention why you are leaving your current employer, but if you do, it should be stated in a way that bolsters your candidacy: "My future certainly would be secure to stay with my current employer, but I am not just interested in security. To be honest with you, they do not have any major new projects planned for me, and I would like a new challenge."

If for any reason you left your last employer under a cloud, go back and negotiate exactly what they will say about you as a reference. This is easier than you think. Nobody wants litigation over your discharge, and the awards escalate rapidly if malice can be shown on the part of the employer. Incidentally, if you want to sue your current or former employer, *get a new job first*. Then sue.

The following two pages show cover letters properly laid out in a conservative, business letter format. The first is a targeted application letter for a management candidate; the second is a broadcast letter for a recent college graduate. Note the strong impression conveyed of the candidates' personalities and work philosophies.

Tara Lynn Johnson

4 White Street, Apt. 5B
New York, New York 10013

Office: (212) 555-2620
Residence: (212) 555-3134

October 18, 1990

Attn: **Human Resources,** Department DK
Re: Position for **Collections Manager,** Tuesday <u>Wall Street Journal</u>, 10/16/90

Dean Witter Reynolds, Inc.
Tower Office, 2 WTC, 73rd Floor
New York, New York 10048

Dear Placement Specialist:

I was very interested to see your advertisement for a Collections Manager. I have long been interested in your company, and this is a position in which I believe I could excel on your behalf. I am enclosing my résumé for your consideration.

As you can see from my résumé, I have advanced accounting and collections experience for a financial services company. My experience spans multistate collection of receivables ranging from small amounts up to $1 million. My authority includes direct negotiation and settlement of receivables, and I work with the company's special counsel for collections on cases as warranted. My greatest collections success, however, has been more organizational in nature: (1) training and motivating collections staff, and (2) making contributions to policy and procedure that have drastically reduced our need to pursue receivables in the first place.

Other strengths include (1) management of accounting staff, (2) design of reporting formats, (3) cash management and cash flow control, (4) operations analysis, and contribution to design of MIS in association with programmer/analysts, and (5) management of human resources administration. These skills may not apply directly to your position, but my experience in these areas will certainly contribute to my ability to perform.

My orientation is toward preventing problems at the point of origination, but I can be quite creative, persistent, and articulate in both logical and persuasive argument to achieve collections goals.

I hope my background will warrant an interview to discuss this further. Please call me. My office is not far from yours, and I would be happy to meet with you at your convenience to see if we can establish a mutual interest.

Yours sincerely,

Tara Lynn Johnson

Tara Lynn Johnson

Enclosure: Résumé.

Salary: Negotiable.

/tj

Margaret Knobloch

6468 Williams Street
Omaha, Nebraska 68106

Telephone / Message:
(402) 555-1707

June 10, 1991

Ms. Lisa Dale Norton
Vice President, Human Resources
U.S. West
110 South 19th Street
Omaha, Nebraska 68106

Dear Ms. Norton:

I am interested in having a short, face-to-face talk with you about
opportunities in telecommunications.

As you can see from the attached, I am a recent college graduate with a
strong liberal arts education. My greatest strengths would have to be my
oral and written communication skills. I am a self-starter. I applied
for and thoroughly enjoyed a year abroad, held several elected offices
in school, and started a local chapter of a national sorority. I have all
the routine office skills, as well as strong organizational abilities as
demonstrated in the internships listed on my résumé.

I would be interested in a customer-service position or other position
involving direct customer contact. Since there are many ways in which I
could serve you, I would like to explore that in a personal meeting.

Even if you don't anticipate any openings, a moment of your time would be
appreciated. I'd like to hear what ideas you have for me.

Thank you so much for your attention. I'll be calling you shortly to see
if we can arrange a time to get together.

Yours sincerely,

Margaret Knobloch

Margaret Knobloch

Customize Your Letters

Anyone at the management level who does not write individual, customized letters is not serious about her job search. Even though you will soon develop a handful of letters that you modify only slightly to use over and over again, each one must be individually typed or word processed and completely free of errors. The typeface on the letter does not have to match the typeface on the résumé. As a matter of fact, a different face confirms the personalized nature of the letter.

If you are not a management candidate, however, there is a shortcut that will work in an emergency. I use this technique with clients who do not have a typewriter, and who simply do not have enough money to manage a proper job search. I write a slightly vague cover letter addressed to the "Prospective Employer," with headings at the top for the date and address. The candidate fills in the date and address neatly by hand.

If the candidate is responding to newspaper advertisements, she cuts the ads out and tapes them onto the top of her cover letter (in addition to writing in the date and addressee by hand). This way the company knows what position she is applying for, and how to route her résumé. Remember, the easier it is to route your résumé, the more likely it will be read by someone who is in a position to give you a job.

The following cover letter demonstrates this generic cover letter approach. This cover letter won the candidate a good position with a law firm, even though she had no legal background. A generic cover letter will not work for a management candidate, but in an emergency it is far better than no cover letter at all.

CASE ASSISTANT
Smart, well org, able to work indpndtly? Track/control complex details of financial lit. 2 yrs. F/T legal exp., exc. writing skills req. NY firm expanding Balt. Great potential. Res. to Valerie Adams, P.O. 12586, Balt., 21210.

Sandy McKie
1602 Lancaster Lane
Baltimore, Maryland 21205
(301) 555-9348

Date:

Attn:

Dear Prospective Employer:

In the interest of exploring employment opportunities within your organization, I have enclosed a copy of my résumé briefly describing my qualifications and credentials.

As my résumé indicates, I have a solid background in administrative services. I have been involved at the supervisory level in the full spectrum of support activities, from directing secretarial staff to administering accounting and billing operations. I have a reputation for dedication and quality performance. I am willing to give an assignment whatever it takes to bring it to fruitful completion.

Please consider me a serious candidate for any administrative position for which I may be qualified. I would like to meet with you to discuss your needs and how I may best be utilized to your success. Please contact me to arrange an interview at your convenience.

Thank you for your consideration. I look forward to our conversation.

Respectfully yours,

Sandy McKie

Enc: Résumé

For some candidates, writing cover letters can be an invitation to disaster. Résumés have a controlled and formulaic style. Cover letters do not, so they can reveal faults that résumés will naturally hide. Bad syntax can come flying out of nowhere. Bad thinking can rear its ugly head. Creative spelling can slip by in your hurry to get the letter in the mail. In general, if you have a good résumé, let it do its job. Keep your cover letters short and to the point, use the telephone, and keep your job search moving along.

If you have any reason to doubt your ability to turn out a large volume of perfect cover letters, you can make a utilitarian cover letter with just an introduction and a call to action. The following cover letter can be used over and over again, if you have a good résumé and the will to use your phone.

> Dear (Ms. or Mr. Next Employer):
>
> In the interest of exploring employment opportunities with you in the area of (you name it), I have enclosed my résumé, briefly describing my qualifications and credentials.
>
> With my experience and background, I am confident that I can make a meaningful and lasting contribution to my next employer. I will be calling you soon to discuss this further, and to see if we can establish a mutual interest.
>
> Please keep my résumé handy, and I can answer any questions you may have when I call. Thank you for your attention, and I look forward to our conversation.
>
> Yours sincerely,
>
> Your Name Here

Once again, do not respond to requests for salary history in a cover letter or any pre-interview communique.

References

Do not provide your references until they are requested, but it is a good idea to know who you would like to use and to ask their permission. I recommend that you send your résumé to your references in advance. This refreshes their memory of how great you are and allows you to prep them on what you want them to say.

Ideally, your references would be your immediate superiors in your last two or three jobs, preferably someone with a direct knowledge of your daily job performance, not a distant CEO who was thrilled with your production figures but had no working knowledge of you.

Incidentally, if you are afraid to send your résumé to your old employers, then it may be inflated. You might want to tone it down to something you know they will endorse.

Peers and subordinates are useless references, as no one will believe them anyway. If you must, you can use vendors, suppliers, or clients of your current company while you are still employed.

Tailor your references to the particular application. For example, if your potential employer seems concerned about your financial skills, your first reference should be able to describe a financial problem you solved or financial project you managed.

If your job search takes a long time, rotate your references, and communicate often with them. The last thing you want is for one of them to become irritated and say to a potential employer, "Jeez, hasn't he gotten a job yet?"

It is not unreasonable to have a very smooth friend call your references, pretending to be a headhunter, and check them out.

A reference listing has the name, current title, current business address, and current daytime telephone of your endorser. If your connection to this reference is not obvious, then state it in parentheses.

Reference:

George Bush
President, United States
(formerly Vice President, United States, when I was a citizen there)

The White House
Washington, D.C. 20500
(202) 456-1414

Chapter 15
Go For It! This Is Your Life

The ability to switch jobs successfully is a talent like any other. It is a talent that can be learned by anybody, and can be improved with practice and study. If you learn this talent well, then you will almost always love your job. Conversely, you will almost never hate your boss, you will be unlikely to feel that your salary is an insult, and you will seldom wonder "what if . . ." for very long before you do something about it.

In the modern job market, your first obligation is to your own career development. If you do not get promotions on a regular basis, then consider a move. If you are not happy, consider a move. My most ambitious clients tell me they expect a promotion every eighteen months or fewer. If they do not get one within that time frame, they will definitely begin the process of switching companies.

I am not recommending that you sacrifice the rest of your life for your career. On the contrary, I am recommending that you have whatever kind of career you want to complement your life as a whole. The principles in this book are sound. They will work to facilitate your career direction, whatever it may be. They can be translated into the nonprofit sector, government service, or the creative arts.

Set your sights high, whatever that means for you. Go for it. This is your life. You are the boss.

Reprinted with permission

Appendix:
Annotated Bibliography of Career Books

The Enemy of Action Is Research!!!!

If you are ready to launch your job search, DO IT NOW and read these books later. Nobody ever learned to swim or play golf by reading a book. You can improve your game by reading these books, but they will only help if you are willing to get wet or slash a few divots first.

SECTION 1: Books on Job Search & Career Advancement Strategies

Books in this section can help you hone a particular skill, such as interviewing or utilizing headhunters effectively. They also can provide far greater understanding of the job search process than is available in this thin volume. However, you should know that the résumé material in many of these books is obsolete, in some cases dangerously obsolete. *Verbum sat sapienti est.*

Reprinted with special permission of Cowles Syndicate, Inc.

Job Search Bibles

The original bible of the job search process is certainly *What Color Is Your Parachute?* by Richard Bolles. This book is revised annually, and anyone who is interested in changing careers, entering the job market, or reentering the job market should definitely read it. I read it every year and learn something new each time.

Another book that has a similar philosophy but is a much quicker read is *Who's Hiring Who*, by Richard Lathrop. This book targets the typical job seeker, and does a good job of explaining the job search process. One does wish it were entitled *Who's Hiring Whom*, however.

If you are a management or professional person pursuing the second, third, or higher rung of your career, I would recommend one of the more comprehensive books. At senior levels, I am downright fond of *Rites of Passage at $100,000+*, by John Lucht. It is one of the most refreshing books on the subject I have read in years, and it comes right from the heart of experience. At more moderate levels, try *The Only Job Hunting Guide You'll Ever Need* or *The Complete Job-Search Handbook*, both satisfyingly comprehensive encyclopedias. Also good are two books by Robert Half, the placement guru: *The Robert Half Way to Get Hired in Today's Job Market*, and *How to Get a Better Job in This Crazy World*.

- *The 1991 What Color is Your Parachute? A practical manual for job-hunters and career-changers.* Richard Nelson Bolles. Berkeley: Ten Speed Press, 1990.

- *Who's Hiring Who? How to find that job fast!* Richard Lathrop. Berkeley: Ten Speed Press, 2nd ed. 1991.
- *Rites of Passage at $100,000+: The insider's guide to absolutely everything about executive job-changing.* John Lucht. New York: The Viceroy Press, 1988.
- *The Only Job Hunting Guide You'll Ever Need: The most comprehensive guide for job hunters and career switchers.* Kathryn and Ross Petras. New York: Poseidon Press, 1988.
- *The Complete Job-Search Handbook: All the skills you need to get any job and have a good time doing it.* Howard Figler, Ph.D. New York: Henry Holt and Co., rev. ed., 1988.
- *How to Get a Better Job in This Crazy World.* Robert Half. New York: Crown Publishers, 1990.
- *The Robert Half Way to Get Hired in Today's Job Market: Get the inside story from the man who has found jobs for over 100,000 people.* Robert Half. New York: Bantam Books, 1983.

Mini Bibles

These two books are great if you only need a quick overview of the job search process. *The Job Search Handbook* is a gem, covering everything from networking to negotiations in just 134 pages. *The Job Hunter's Final Exam* is less comprehensive, but an even quicker read. The scoring is frustratingly arbitrary, however, so do not think you are unemployable if you get a poor grade. I would recommend you take the job exam for fun after you have read one or more other books.

- *The Job Search Handbook: The basics of a professional job search.* John Noble. Boston: Bob Adams, 1988.
- *The Job Hunter's Final Exam: With all the answers.* Thomas M. Camden. Chicago: Surrey Books, 1990.

Don't Know What You Want to Do Next?

The exercises in *What Color is Your Parachute* (described above), *Where Do I Go From Here With My Life,* and *Discover What You're Best At* are fun if you take the right approach. Be disciplined, follow the instructions, and go through these books one step at a time. *Wishcraft* and *The Three Boxes of Life* are more philosophical in their approach than the first three books, but for some people that will work better. Finally, *Before You Say "I Quit!"* is a book I would recommend to anyone who is itching to quit, but has not decided what to do next. It is a quick and perceptive primer, and just may teach you how to become happy with the job you already have.

- *Where Do I Go From Here with My Life?: A very systematic, practical, and effective life/work planning manual for students of all ages, instructors, counselors, career seekers, and career changers.* John C. Crystal and Richard Nelson Bolles. Berkeley: Ten Speed Press, 1974.
- *Discover What You're Best At: The national career aptitude system and career directory.* Barry and Linda Gale. New York: Simon & Schuster, 1982.
- *Wishcraft: How to get what you really want.* Barbara Sher, with Annie Gottlieb. New York: Ballantine Books, rev. ed. 1983.
- *The Three Boxes of Life and how to get out of them: An introduction to life/work planning.* Richard N. Bolles. Berkeley: Ten Speed Press, rev. ed., 1981.
- *Do What You Love, the Money will Follow: Discovering your right livelihood.* Marsha Sinetar. New York: Dell Publishing, 1987.
- *Before You Say "I Quit!": A guide to making successful job transitions.* Diane Holloway, Ph.D., and Nancy Bishop. New York: Collier Books, 1990.
- *Work with Passion: How to do what you love for a living.* Nancy Anderson. New York: Carroll & Graf, 1986.

Cover Letters

If you need additional cover letter guidance, *200 Letters for Job-Hunters* is the new bible in this department. *Dynamic Cover Letters* is a quick overview. *The Perfect Cover Letter* is also good.

- *200 Letters for Job-Hunters: Every possible way to get job offers.* William Frank. Berkeley: Ten Speed Press, 1990.
- *Dynamic Cover Letters: How to sell yourself to an employer by writing a letter that will get your resume read, get you an interview...and get you a job!* Katharine Hansen, with Randall Hansen. Berkeley: Ten Speed Press, 1990.
- *The Perfect Cover Letter.* Richard H. Beatty. New York: John Wiley & Sons, 1989.

Interviewing

I heavily recommend that you read at least one interviewing book sometime early in your job search. *Sweaty Palms* is a quicker read and covers all the bases sufficiently; *Knock 'Em Dead* is more thorough. My favorite business book of all time is *How to Win Friends & Influence People,* by Dale Carnegie. Do not let the Machiavellian title fool you; this book should be renamed "Business Etiquette 101," or "How to Be Nice to Everybody and Win." If you have never read it, you will enjoy it, and you will learn something to make your next human interaction more successful. (Carnegie's book has sold over fifteen million copies; your next boss has almost certainly read it.) Finally, the interview section of *Hot Tips, Sneaky Tricks & Last-Ditch Tactics* has material that is not found in any other book.

- *Sweaty Palms: The Neglected Art of Being Interviewed.* H. Anthony Medley. Berkeley: Ten Speed Press, 1985.
- *Knock 'em Dead: With great answers to tough interview questions.* Martin John Yate. Boston: Bob Adams, 1990.
- *How to Win Friends & Influence People.* Dale Carnegie. New York: Pocket Books, rev. ed., 1981.
- *Hot Tips, Sneaky Tricks & Last-Ditch Tactics: An insider's guide to getting your first corporate job.* Jeff B. Speck. New York: John Wiley & Sons, 1989.

Undergraduate or M.B.A. Student?

Hot Tips, Sneaky Tricks & Last-Ditch Tactics (decribed above) is targeted to students who use the on-campus corporate interviewing process to get a first job. Whereas I have encouraged you to show the most flattering side of the truth, this book actually encourages you to bend it. Be careful. That aside, this is a refreshingly different career book, told from the corporate recruiter's point of view of all those on-campus interviews. This book is neck deep in good advice, and it is fun to read.

Headhunters

Rites of Passage (described above) is the best book on retainer firms and strategies for the job search at six figures and up. *The Headhunter Strategy* has a shrewd explanation of the industry, and offers the reader a comprehensive approach for using executive search consultants in a management-level job search. *The Directory of Executive Recruiters* is the best directory on both contingency and retainer firms, and it comes complete with a hundred pages of "user's manual" explaining how to contact and interact with search consultants. The *Directory* lists the firms themselves, including key principals, addresses, and areas of specialty. You can also call Kenneth J. Cole at (800) 634-4548 or (904) 235-3733 and buy a custom printout sorted to your specifications by industry, functional specialty, and geographic area. *How to Get a Headhunter to Call* and *Hunting the Headhunters* do just what their titles suggest.

- *The Headhunter Strategy: How to make it work for you.* Kenneth J. Cole. New York: John Wiley & Sons, 1985.

- *The Directory of Executive Recruiters.* Fitzwilliam, N. H.: Kennedy Publications. (annual, call (603) 585-2200 or (603) 585-6544 to order by phone).
- *How to Get a Headhunter to Call.* Howard Freedman. New York: John Wiley & Sons, 1986.
- *Hunting the Headhunters: A woman's guide.* Diane Cole. New York: Simon & Schuster, 1988.

Telephone Technique

Telesearch is one of those out-of-print books that really shouldn't be. It provides an effective telephone-based job-search strategy and has a great collection of tips on using the telephone effectively for any business purpose. It is without question a unique and valuable resource, and worth a trip to your library to see if they have it.

- *Telesearch: Direct dial the best job of your life. The most effective job hunting guide you'll ever find.* John Truitt. New York: Collier Books, 1985. O.P.

Functional Résumés

There is only one source: Yana Parker.

- *The Damn Good Resume Guide: Say goodbye to your old lifeless resumes, say hello to sharp, effective resumes.* Yana Parker. Berkeley: Ten Speed Press, rev. ed., 1989.
- *The Resume Catalog: 200 damn good examples.* Yana Parker. Berkeley: Ten Speed Press, 1988.

If You Don't Understand the Modern Job Market

These books are a little dated, but they demonstrate in detail the rationale for thinking of yourself as a marketable product rather than a beggar for a job.

- *Guerrilla Tactics in the Job Market.* Tom Jackson. New York: Bantam Books, 1978.
- *Go Hire Yourself an Employer.* Richard K. Irish. New York: Anchor Press, rev. ed., 1987.

SECTION 2: How to Do Research on Companies

People who find this topic mysterious are usually the same people who have never set foot in the reference section of their city's library. The reference librarians are there to help you, and you can bet they will if you already know what to ask for. The books in this section are a good place to start. Remember to build a big lead list and contact several companies simultaneously, not just one at a time.

Also, if you are interested in a major corporation, call its investor relations department and tell them you are interested in investing in their company (which is true) or just say that you will soon have an appointment with someone in the company and you want to be informed for the meeting (which is also true). Ask for any general and financial information they may have. If the company does not have an investor relations department, ask for the corporate communications department or the public relations department. If you do not want to call the company yourself, my stockbroker would be happy to handle this for you; call Eric Schwaab at (212) 392-7681 or (800) 776-4477.

Unless you are an accountant or analyst, do not worry too much about the financial information. You want to know what the company does, where it came from, and where it thinks it is going. The company's own material will tell you clearly. If you want to review the financials, read Tracy's *How to Read a Financial Report*.

Also, it is a good idea to check *Who's Who* to see what information you can find on top officers. Maybe your interviewer is in there too—you never know.

Finally, check your local business press for articles in the last six months, and check the national business press through the *Business Periodicals Index*.

General Guides

- *The 100 Best Companies to Work For in America*. Robert Levering, et al. New York: New American Library, 1987.
- *The Best Companies for Women*. Baila Zeitz, Ph.D., and Lorraine Dusky. New York: Simon and Schuster, 1988.
- *How to Read a Financial Report*. John A. Tracy. New York: Wiley & Sons, 1980.

Periodicals

- *America's Corporate Families* (formerly *Billion Dollar Directory*). Mountain Lakes, N.J.: Dun & Bradstreet.
- *Directory of Corporate Affiliations*. Wilmette, Ill.: National Register Publishing Company.
- *Corporate 1000 and International Corporate 1000*. Washington, D.C.: Monitor Publishing.
- *Encyclopedia of Business Information Sources*. Detroit: Gale Research. Biannual.
- *Directories in Print* (formerly *Directory of Directories*). Detroit: Gale Research.
- *Encyclopedia of Associations*. Detroit: Gale Research.
- *Guide to American Directories*. Coral Springs, Fla.: B. Klein Publications. Biannual.
- *Business Periodicals Index*. Bronx: Wilson Publishing.
- *Commerce Register's Geographical Directories of Manufacturers* (for various locales and metropolitan regions nationwide). Midland Park, N. J.: Commerce Register.
- *Thomas' Register of American Manufacturers*. New York: Thomas Publishing.
- *State Manufacturing Directories*. Vary by state, but every state has one.
- *Reference Book of Corporate Managements*. Parsippany, N.J.: Dun & Bradstreet.
- *Ward's Business Directory*. Belmont, Ca.: Information Access.
- *Million Dollar Directory Series*. Parsippany, N.J.: Dun & Bradstreet.
- *Standard Directory of Advertisers* (by product and by location). Wilmette, Ill.: National Register Publishing Company.
- *Standard & Poor's Register of Corporations, Directors, & Executives*. New York: Standard & Poor.
- *Who's Who in America*. Wilmette, Ill.: Marquis Who's Who.
- *Who's Who in Finance & Industry*. Wilmette, Ill.: Marquis Who's Who.
- *National Directory of Addresses and Telephone Numbers*. Kirkland, Wash.: General Information.
- *Yellow Pages*. Note: Some airports and libraries have telephone directories from every major U.S. city.

Specific Guides (a few examples)

- *Aerospace Companies*. Greenwich, Conn.: DMS, Inc.
- *American Apparel Manufacturers Association Directory*. Arlington, Va.: AAMA.
- *American Electronics Association Directory*. Palo Alto, Ca.: AEA.
- *The Biotechnology Directory*. New York: Stockton Press.
- *Broadcasting/Cablecasting Yearbook*. Washington, D.C.: Broadcasting Publications, Inc.
- *Chain Store Guides* (numerous). New York: Business Guides Inc. (212) 371-9400.
- *Chemical Industry Directory*. New York: State Mutual Book and Periodical Service, Ltd.
- *Data Sources—The Comprehensive Guide to the Information Processing Industry*. New York: Ziff-Davis.
- *Directory of Hotel and Motel Systems*. New York: American Hotel Association Directory Corp.

- *Insurance Almanac.* Englewood, N.J.: Underwriter Printing and Publishing.
- *International Directory of Marketing Research Houses* (aka *The Green Book*). New York: American Marketing Association.
- *National Roster of Realtors Directory.* Cedar Rapids, Iowa: Stamats Communications, Inc.
- *Rand McNally International Bankers Directory.* Chicago: Rand McNally.
- *Telephone Industry Directory & Source Book.* Potomac, Mich.: Phillips Publishing.
- *Working Press of the Nation.* Burlington, Iowa: National Research Bureau.
- *World Directory of Pharmaceutical Manufacturers.* London: IMS World Publications.

Acknowledgements

Many special thanks to Kathleen Docherty. Many special thanks to Jordana Soares. Special thanks to Ten Speed Press: Phil, George, Sal, Mariah, and Maureen. Special thanks to Merlyn M. Bell, for giving me the title to this book. Special thanks to Prof. Walter Englert, Classics Department, Reed College, and to Apuleius, for the résumé selections in Latin from *The Golden Ass.* Special thanks to Stan Shpetner from Georgetown University for his research assistance. Special thanks to Rebecca Lemov from Yale University for her copyediting expertise. The errors are all mine, but many, many people have contributed to this book. Thank you all.

ALSO BY DONALD ASHER:

Graduate Admissions Essays—What Works, What Doesn't, and Why

The author of *Overnight Resume* checks in with effective writing techniques that will allow anyone to craft an impressive essay—overnight. Based on interviews with admissions officers at top schools, it includes samples of *their* favorites. $9.95 paper, 128 pages

From College to Career: Entry Level Resumes for Any Major

Real-world examples illustrate techniques for showing any academic or job experience (or lack thereof) in the best light. $7.95 paper, 128 pages

. . . AND MORE HELP FOR THE JOB HUNTER:

Dynamic Cover Letters by Katherine Hansen

Too often, people put all of their creative energy into writing a great resume, and then send it off with a lackluster cover letter. The savvy marketing tips, simple charts and exercises, and over fifty examples of real letters in this book allow anyone to create a dynamic, effective cover letter. $7.95 paper, 96 pages

What Color Is Your Parachute? by Richard N. Bolles

This classic in the career field is substantially revised and updated every year. Practical advice, step-by-step exercises, and a warm, human tone make it *the* guide for job-hunters and career changers. "The giant title in the field"—*New York Times* $12.95 paper, 425 pages

How to Create a Picture of Your Ideal Job or Next Career by Richard N. Bolles

This workbook, taken from *Parachute*, helps job-hunters identify the skills they most enjoy using, and the work setting which will be most satisfying. Covers long- and short-term planning, salary negotiation, and other important issues. $4.95 paper, 64 pages

Sweaty Palms by H. Anthony Medley

One of the most popular books ever on job interviewing, fully revised and updated for the 90s. Tells how to prepare for an interview, answer difficult or illegal questions, and leave a great impression. Special sections on dealing with discrimination or harassment. $9.95 paper, 194 pages

Available from your local bookstore, or order direct from the publisher. Please include $1.25 shipping & handling for the first book, and 50 cents for each additional book. California residents include local sales tax. Write for our free complete catalog of over 400 books and tapes.

Ship to:
Name_____
Address _____
City _____ State _____ Zip _____
Phone: (_____) _____

TEN SPEED PRESS
P.O. Box 7123
Berkeley, CA 94707
For VISA or Mastercard orders call (510) 845-8414